GOOD NEWS STUDIES

Consulting Editor: Robert J. Karris, O.F.M.

Volume 29

Jesus and His Towns

by

Sherman E. Johnson

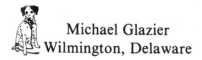

Michael Glazier
Wilmington, Delaware

About the Author

Sherman Johnson is currently Dean Emeritus at the Church Divinity School of the Pacific. He received his Ph.D. in 1936 from the University of Chicago. He has taught New Testament in various seminaries and his archaeological work has taken him to most of the places described in this book. Among his many publications is *Paul the Apostle & His Cities* (Michael Glazier, 1987).

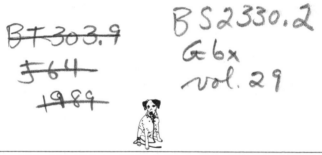

First published in 1989 by Michael Glazier, Inc., 1935 West Fourth Street, Wilmington, Delaware 19805.

Library of Congress Cataloging-in-Publication Data

Johnson, Sherman E. (Sherman Elbridge), 1908-Jesus and His Towns.

(Good news studies; v. 29)

1. Jesus Christ—Journeys. 2. Cities and towns—Palestine. 3. Palestine—Description and travel.
I. Title. II. Series.
BT303.9.J64 1988 226/.091 88-33408
ISBN: 0-89453-653-2

Typography by Phyllis Boyd LeVane
Printed in the United States of America by Edwards Brothers

To the Glory of God
and in Honor of Three Jerusalem Institutions
St. George's College
École Biblique et Archeologique
Ecumenical Institute, Tantur

Contents

Preface

There are so many guide books to the Holy Land and works on the life and teaching of Jesus—some of them of high quality—that it is best to explain why the present volume came to be written. One reason is that I do not know of a book with exactly the same scope and purpose; the other is that I found pleasure in writing it.

This is primarily for persons who have more than a casual interest, both historical and religious, in the life and times of Jesus, who may contemplate a pilgrimage to the Holy Land or who have visited it and wish to know more about what they have seen. It is not restricted to these; one hopes that those who do not go at all will profit from the book.

The several chapters are organized around places and itineraries in the gospel story. My own experience, from having been in the Holy Land several times and sometimes for long periods, from the last days of the British Mandate until a few years ago, is that to know the geography of this fascinating part of the earth makes the gospel story more concrete and vivid.

Nearly all of Jesus' cities and villages figure in many periods of history. Thus I pay some attention to the history and culture of Old Testament times, the days of the early Church, the Middle Ages, and more recent centuries. Archaeological discoveries are mentioned when they are relevant. Finally I discuss various parts of the gospels in their geographical setting, although this does not attempt to be a complete discussion of Jesus' life and teaching.

This book is therefore a companion volume to *Paul the Apostle and His Cities* and is built on somewhat the same plan.

When handling materials in the Bible I have made full use of the modern methods of biblical study. I believe that Scripture needs to be read as a collection of historical sources, and *in context*, with full attention to the cultural background of each part. At the same time, I write as a churchman, as a member of the community of faith, and the reader will not fail to discern that my literary journey through the sacred sites is more than an historical exercise.

I have had the privilege of knowing many archaeologists and historians of the Holy Land, some of whose books will appear in the bibliography. Especial use has been made of two excellent guide books, *The Jerusalem Jesus Knew*, by John Wilkinson, and *The Holy Land: An Archaeological Guide from Earliest Times to 1700*, by Jerome Murphy-O'Connor, O.P. These works give fuller information on many points discussed here, and their distinguished authors are not responsible for any errors I may have committed.

Quotations from the Old Testament are from the Revised Standard Version, except for instances where another version is indicated. New Testament quotations are my own translation unless a version is specified.

Photographs were provided through the courtesy of the American Bible Society, with the exception of the view of Plowing and Sowing at Bethshemesh, furnished by the author.

Special thanks are due to Michael Glazier for his friendly encouragement of this work, and for suggestions made by his editors.

Sherman E. Johnson

1

Bethlehem

I

We begin with Bethlehem because the gospels of Matthew and Luke say that Jesus was born there.

Our mental picture of Bethlehem was probably first formed by Christmas pageants—for younger people, what they saw on television—and from carols and hymns: "Once in royal David's city," "Earth has many a noble city,/ Bethlehem, thou dost all excel," and of course "O little town of Bethlehem," which Phillips Brooks wrote for Trinity Church, Boston. Along with all this, we heard the Christmas stories from the gospels.

One who visits modern Bethlehem sees a different town. It has grown up, more or less, into the 20th century. Sometimes it is startling, but behind this place whose inhabitants have to make a living and carry on all their daily occupations, it is still possible to imagine the city as it was in the time of Jesus.

There have been many Bethlehems, or rather such a city has gone through several phases—in prehistory, in the time of Ruth and David, the period of Herod, the Muslim invasion, the Crusades, the Turkish empire, and the present century. With the help of history we can contemplate it through a variety of lenses. Sometimes it helps to see old drawings, such as the lithographs David Roberts made in the 1830s. These, to be sure, do not portray the Bethlehem of

Jesus but show it as it was before modern European life touched it.

II

Bethlehem was a desirable place for human habitation, and this is proved by the fact that it was occupied as early as the Old Stone Age (before 10,000 B.C.). Present-day residents proudly claim that it is one of the most healthful cities in the Holy Land.

Bethlehem first comes into recorded history in the 14th century B.C., in cuneiform tablets consisting of correspondence that were found at Tell el-Amarna in Egypt, south of Cairo. At that time Egypt had lost much of its previous control over Palestine. Amenhotep IV became so interested in religion that he did little to maintain his power in the northern part of his empire. He replaced worship of the god Amen with the exclusive cult of the sun-disk Aton and changed his own name to Akhenaton or Ikhnaton, and he may have been author of the Hymn to Aton which seems almost to be monotheistic (see *Ancient Near Eastern Texts*, pp. 365-370).

Egypt's vassal princes in Palestine and Syria wrote these letters to the Pharaoh's court complaining that wandering hordes of people called Apiru or Habiru had taken control of part of their territory, and they asked military help and advice.

One of these was Abdi-Heba or Abdi-Khepa, ruler of Jerusalem. He wanted assistance in regaining Bit-Laḥmi, which had gone over to the Habiru.

So at that early date Bethlehem had the name it bears today. The Hebrew form of the name, Beth-leḥem, seems to mean "house of bread," and the related Arabic name Beit-laḥm can be understood as "house of meat." Scholars guess, however, that originally it included the name of a long forgotten god Laḥmi. We ourselves like the popular derivation "house of bread," for it suggests Jesus giving bread to the hungry and Ruth gleaning in the barley fields of Bethlehem.

III

Jews and Christians come back to Bethlehem for prayer and spiritual refreshment. Just so Ruth, the Moabite widow, found not only a home but also the worship of God when she accompanied her mother-in-law back to Naomi's home town. "Entreat me not to leave you or to return from following you; for where you go I will go, and where you lodge I will lodge; your people shall be my people, and your God my God; where you die, I will die, and there will I be buried. May the Lord do so to me and more also if even death parts me from you" (Ruth 1:16-17). She made a happy marriage with Boaz and became the ancestress of King David.

One wonders where these barley fields were. They might be a little east of Bethlehem, near the village of Beit Sahur, but another local tradition places them west of Bethlehem.

IV

Ruth and Boaz lived in the time of the Judges. Their story gives an impression of peace and happiness, but the Book of Judges shows that this could have been only a pleasant interlude in an era of turmoil. The Israelite tribes were only gradually getting control of the Promised Land; they had not yet coalesced into a nation, and even their religion was half pagan. The "judges" were leaders who arose from time to time and won temporary victories over Canaanites, Midianites, Amalekites, Ammonites and Philistines—a variety of enemies, Arabs from the south, old dwellers on both sides of the Jordan, and the Philistines who may have come from the Greek islands.

Bethlehem comes into the story because of an unnamed Levite who lived there (Judg. 17-18). A man named Micah from the hill country of Ephraim in the north took a quantity of silver and had a "graven and molten image" made from it, and also an ephod and teraphin. "Ephod" can mean several things; sometimes it is a cultic garment; here it may refer to an image or to an object used in consulting an oracle. The teraphim were images, sometimes of household gods. Micah lived at a time when many Israelites were still half-pagan in their practices, and images were contrary to the Mosaic law (Exod. 20:4, 23). Furthermore, Micah had chosen one of his sons to be his priest, but when the Levite arrived he hired him for that office. Now Micah was sure that the Lord would help him.

But this happy arrangement was not to last long. The tribe of Dan was looking for a new place to settle, and on their way north some of the Danites came upon the Levite and carried him off with the sacred objects to Laish, near the sources of the Jordan. There they set up the image and founded the new city of Dan.

The Book of Judges concludes with a series of events that show what an unruly time this was. The brutal murder of a woman from Bethlehem by men of the tribe of Benjamin led to the slaughter of many men of the tribe. The other Israelites refused to let their daughters marry into this tribe, and finally the Benjaminite men seized women who were celebrating a festival at Shiloh (Judg. 19-21).

V

Nine centuries before the time of Jesus, David made Bethlehem famous. The stories about him and his predecessor King Saul illustrate how parts of the Old Testament were written, for they seem to combine a "Rise of David Source" and a "Succession Narrative." The unknown scribe who composed the First Book of Samuel wove them together, but in such a way as to preserve both traditions. Because of his fidelity to his sources we are able to distinguish an earlier contemporary account from the Succession Narrative which glorifies David to a greater degree.

Saul, the first king after the period of the Judges, began the difficult task of liberating the Hebrews from the Philistines. These people, from whom Palestine takes its name, were pagans and part of the "sea peoples" who are known from Egyptian records to have conquered the seacoast. They settled there, at Shiloh they seized the Ark of the Covenant, the wooden chest which the Israelites used in worship, and dominated much of the Holy Land.

Saul was a tall young man from the tribe of Benjamin who on one occasion went out looking for his father's lost donkeys. In hope of finding them he consulted Samuel, who was a "seer" or prophet. Samuel not only disclosed that the asses had already been found, but also as directed by an oracle from Yahweh anointed Saul as king of Israel (1 Sam. 9:17; 10:1-8), and encouraged him to fight the Philistines. This is in the Rise of David source, which is favorable to Saul.

His reign was only a partial success. Saul was emotionally unstable; he came to have an insane jealousy of David and tried to kill him. At last he and his son Jonathan were slain in battle at Mt. Gilboa near the Jezreel valley. In contrast, David succeeded in defeating the Philistines, recovering the Ark, and establishing a firm kingdom. Therefore the belief grew up that it had always been God's purpose to make David the king, but according to the Succession Narrative, Samuel taught that the nation should have no king but God himself. It was only because the people had demanded an earthly monarch that the prophet asked God to provide one (1 Sam. 10:17-24; Chap. 12).

The two sources also have different stories of how David came into Saul's service. Both tell of David's encounter with Goliath, but in the Rise Source David was chosen to be Saul's armor bearer because the king suffered from depression ("an evil spirit from Yahweh tormented him," I Sam. 16:14), and David was skilled in playing the lyre. Whenever he made music for Saul the king recovered.

Few stories in Scripture are as moving and religiously meaningful as the one in which Samuel was led to anoint David as the future king. Jesse's seven sons are introduced to the prophet, but none of them is chosen, and David has to be brought in from herding the sheep (I Sam. 16:1-13). "The Lord sees not as man sees; man looks on the outward appearance, but the Lord looks on the heart" (16:7).

The actor Charles Laughton's famous recording of the next episode (1 Sam. 17) brings out the dramatic power of the story. It is only the shepherd boy who has the courage to meet Goliath of Gath and slay him with a stone from his sling. This was in the valley of Elah, in the foothill country between the central range and the coastal plain.

As one of Saul's military commanders, David won other victories over the Philistines, and these led Saul to be jealous and suspicious. For a long time David was a fugitive and even took service temporarily under Achish, the Philistine king of Gath. But after the death of Saul the "elders of Israel" appointed him king. This was at Hebron, where he reigned for seven years and six months over Judah (2 Sam. 5:1-5). When later he established his sovereignty over the northern tribes he was shrewd enough to make Jerusalem his capital. This was on the border between Judah and Benjamin and belonged to no tribe. He had captured it himself from the local Jebusites.

One charming story tells of a time when the Philistines were garrisoned in Bethlehem itself, and David longed for a drink of water from the well near the city gate. Three brave soldiers broke through the camp, drew the water and brought it to David. But he poured it out as an offering to Yahweh. "Far be it from me, O Lord, that I should do this. Shall I drink the blood of the men who went at the risk of their lives?" (2 Sam. 23:13-17). On the north side of Bethlehem pilgrims are shown a well which local piety has claimed to be David's well.

Because of David's reputation as a musician and singer, the Psalms came to be ascribed to him. He may have written at least one of them (Ps. 18). One of the collection in that book, called "Psalms of David," could have been composed during the monarchy he established. Later he became an ideal figure, particularly in First Chronicles, and he was the inspiration for the hope of a Messiah, an anointed king descended from him (see especially Isa. 9:2-7; 11:1-9). This was not the only concept of Messiah in Judaism, but it is evidently the earliest and most enduring one.

We have to be grateful that someone preserved the historical traditions that exhibit his human failings. He could be angry and unjust on occasion, and he was a man of powerful emotions. When his son Absalom revolted against him, he still loved the young man and mourned his death so bitterly that his officers felt insulted (2 Sam. 18:19—19:8). No one can excuse David for his adultery with Bathsheba and his sending of her husband Uriah to death in battle, but David's repentance was genuine (2 Sam. 12:1-23).

VI

When Nebuchadnezzar invaded Jerusalem for a second time in 586 B.C., and David's monarchy came to an end, people from Bethlehem were deported along with many others from all parts of Judah. We are told that some seventy years later, 123 men from Bethlehem returned from exile in Babylonia.

Bethlehem continued to be the focus of hope. An oracle preserved in Micah 5:2-4 recalls David and Matt. 2:6 quotes it as a promise of Jesus:

> But you, O Bethlehem Ephrathah,
>   who are little to be among the clans of Judah,
> from you shall come forth for me
>   one who is to be ruler in Israel,
> whose origin is from of old,
>   from ancient days.

The word "messiah" means anointed, and although prophets and priests were anointed, "Messiah" right down to the time of Jesus referred especially to a king descended from David. Hymns known as the *Psalms of Solomon* were written in a time of misery not long after Pompey the Great captured Jerusalem in 63 B.C., and one of these, just after speaking of God's People, contains this prayer:

> Hearken, Lord, and raise up for them their king, son of
> David,
> for the time which you yourself, God, have seen, to reign
> over Israel your servant (Ps. Sol. 17:23).

An earlier verse of the same psalm reads:

> We shall hope in God our Saviour,
> because the might of our God is forever with mercy,
> and the reign of our God is forever over the nations.

VII

Christians regard the nativity of Jesus in that city as Bethlehem's greatest glory, and traditionally they have thought it the fulfilment of all such prophecies.

Matthew and Luke locate Jesus' birth in Bethlehem. If we had only Mark and John we might suppose that Jesus had been born in Nazareth. The gospels regularly call him the Nazarene (*Nazarenos* in Mark and Luke, *Nazoraios* in Matthew, Luke and John), and when Mark speaks of our Lord's home village he no doubt means Nazareth.

There is in fact another village named Bethlehem. It is in Galilee, perhaps seven miles from Nazareth, west and a little north, and has the same Arabic name, *Beit Lahm*. So far as I know, no one has seriously proposed that this was where Jesus was born. Luke 2:4 locates the nativity in "the city of David called Bethlehem," and in Matt. 2:1 it is "Bethlehem of Judah."

In Luke, the annunciation to Mary takes place in Nazareth, but if we had only Matthew, it would be more natural to suppose that it was at Bethlehem. What the angel Gabriel tells Mary is a perfect example of the messianic language of the Old Testament: "He shall be great and called son of the Most High, and the Lord God will give him the throne of David his ancestor, and he will reign over the house of Jacob forever, and of his kingdom there will be no end" (Luke 1:32-33). Indeed the hymns that we call *Magnificat* (1:46-55),

Benedictus (1:68-79) and *Nunc Dimittis* (2:29-32) are some-what like Old Testament psalms, and Mary's song is model-led on that of Hannah (1 Sam. 2:1-10). But it is also striking that they contain phrases similar to those in the Psalms of Solomon. These were hymns written not far from 63 B.C., when Pompey the Great invaded Jerusalem, deposed the Maccabaean ruler, and put Palestine under Roman rule. The author prayed for a future king from the house of David.

VIII

We do not know where Luke found the traditions in his story of Jesus' birth. There are historical problems. When a census was taken, people were usually enrolled in their usual domiciles, not their ancestral homes (Luke 2:3), and Luke's chronology is confused. Jesus could not have been about thirty years old at the beginning of his ministry (3:23) if he was born about the time when Quirinius, the legate of Syria, took a census in A.D. 6. This was when Herod's son Ar-chelaus was deposed and Judaea became part of the Roman empire.

Luke, in telling of the Nativity, perhaps had in mind Jeremiah's prayer in which he asks why God should be "like a stranger in the land, like a wayfarer who turns aside to tarry for a night" (Jer. 14:8), and the words of Isa. 1:3, "The ox knows its owner, and the ass its master's crib." He has, in any case, told a deathless and charming story of how in David's city, where there was no room in the inn or guest-chamber, Jesus was born in a manger.

As early as the 2nd century A.D. there was a tradition that this manger was in a cave. When the Christian Church at last had its liberty under Constantine in the early 4th century, that emperor had a church built, with an octagonal apse, over the traditional grotto. Queen Helena dedicated it in 332. St. Cyril of Jerusalem tells us that this was in a grove that had been dedicated to the god Tammuz or Adonis since the time of the emperor Hadrian (117-138). We know that Hadrian built a temple to the Roman gods over the Holy Sepulchre in Jerusalem.

St. Jerome lived here for many years and made the spot a monastic centre. One of the caves is traditionally his study, where he made a complete translation of the Scriptures into Latin (the Vulgate) and wrote other books. The church was rebuilt by Justinian in the 6th century, but excavations have disclosed the outline of the original church.

When the Persians invaded Palestine in 614 and destroyed many churches, the Bethlehem church was spared because a mosaic on the facade portrayed the Magi in Persian dress. In the Crusader period the roof was restored and work was done on the interior decorations. Since then the building has undergone few changes.

A passageway beneath the apse leads to the grotto below. A star set into the pavement marks the traditional spot of the Nativity. There is access to the grotto from the other side, and a stairway descends from the Latin (Roman Catholic) church of St. Catherine, which was built in 1881.

The Church of the Nativity has always been an Orthodox church except in Crusader times, and is under the Greek patriarchate of Jerusalem. Other ancient churches have traditional rights to worship there, and at times like Christmas the Eucharist may be celebrated at a side altar while the Orthodox liturgy is going on.

The Gospel of Luke speaks only of an inn or lodging place and mentions no cave. This is perhaps not strange, because there are houses in Bethlehem built into caves. A very comfortable tourist pavilion at Petra in Jordan is integrated into a grotto which serves as one of the public rooms. In the Turkish period, at least, an inn (khan or caravanserai) usually consisted of sleeping rooms built around a courtyard in which horses, donkeys and vehicles of the travellers were kept. For reasons of security there was only one entrance to the complex. The Büyük Khan at Nicosia in Cyprus is an elegant example of such a place.

Luke could not have been thinking of an elaborate building like this. It was probably a simple structure with one or more rooms. The cave at the rear was for the animals, and the manger may have been carved from the rock. Villagers like Joseph and Mary were used to living simply, but this was

Bethlehem

somewhat more spartan, and Luke expresses the pathos in a
few words. Later, when the boy grew up, he was to say,
"Foxes have lairs and the birds of the sky have nests, but the
Son of Man has no place to lay his head" Matt. 8:20).

IX

Bethlehem lies about four miles south of the Old City of
Jerusalem. After 1948, under Jordanian administration, it
required a trip of about ten miles on a winding road to go

there from East Jerusalem. Since the 1967 war, when Israel conquered the West Bank, it has been possible to take the direct route. The south boundary of the Jerusalem municipality is rather close to Bethlehem. After one passes the Ecumenical Institute at Tantur on the right, Bethlehem comes into full view, lying on a hill and its northern slopes.

The reputed tomb of Rachel is on this road. Gen. 35:19 states that Rachel was "buried on the way to Ephrath (that is, Bethlehem)," but the tradition in I Sam. 10:2 may be correct; Jacob's beloved wife was buried in the territory of Benjamin, north of Jerusalem.

Beyond Rachel's Tomb one comes to the French Hospital, and now the road curves southeast toward the broad Manger Square, the heart of the city, where the basilica of the Nativity is located.

The structures of Bethlehem have great variety. Many of the older houses are of Turkish or Arab type, as in Jerusalem's Old City. The churches and convents are in Greek Byzantine or neo-Gothic style, some of them built in the 19th and 20th centuries. The churches represent various denominations, Latin Catholic, Greek Catholic, Greek Orthodox, Armenian, Coptic and Lutheran.

Since the wars of 1948 and 1967, so many Muslims have found homes in the city that they are now a majority of the population, and there are several mosques here. Before 1948 Bethlehem was almost entirely Christian.

The ancient basilica and St. Catherine's Church are at the northeast of Manger Square. Nearby are a Latin guest hostel and Greek and Armenian convents. The shops on the square cater to pilgrims and tourists and offer a variety of souvenirs made of olive wood and mother of pearl. When the first of the Dead Sea Scrolls were discovered in 1947, some of them were brought to an antiquities dealer in Bethlehem.

After telling of Jesus' birth, Luke goes on to say, "There were shepherds in that same country living outdoors and keeping watch over their flocks by night," and it was then that they heard the news from an angel of the Lord that a Saviour had been born in the city of David. This was followed by the *Gloria in Excelsis* sung by the heavenly choir, whereupon they went to Bethlehem and visited the manger. "And Mary paid careful attention to all these matters and pondered them in her mind" (Luke 2:8-20).

Luke's scene conforms to the geography. Near Bethlehem rainfall is fairly good, and wheat and barley can be cultivated, but as one goes east the rains diminish quickly. The steppe country permits some marginal agriculture, but finally as one approaches the Dead Sea region the country is sheer desert. Sheep and goats have always been herded in this steppe, and to this day the Ta'amireh tribe of Beduin, who discovered the first Dead Sea Scrolls, roam from the desert as far as the Bethlehem neighborhood. At least until recently shepherds and their flocks could be seen in east Jerusalem.

It was natural for Christians to identify a "Shepherds' Field" and to make their devotions there. There are three such places, all near the Christian village of Beit Sahur, a mile or so east of Bethlehem. The oldest is near the Greek Orthodox Church; adjoining it is a small chapel adorned with frescoes. In modern times Latin Catholics have established another field, and a little farther east is a field dedicated by the YMCA, where Protestant pilgrims sing carols on Christmas Eve. Still another field is pointed out as the one belonging to Boaz, where Ruth gleaned.

X

Matthew tells how the "magi," wise men or astrologers, came to search for the child born to be king of the Jews. Such men could have come from Babylonia or Persia. They said that they had seen the star, perhaps while they were "in the east," but the Greek phrase could mean "at its rising" at sunrise. Ancient people, like many moderns, believed that the heavenly bodies determined destiny and foretold important events.

It is impossible to know for certain what star is referred to in the gospel. One popular theory connects this with Halley's comet, which was seen in 12 B.C., another with the conjunction of Jupiter and Saturn in 7 B.C., which would produce the effect of an unusually bright star. But more probably the evangelist thought of the prophecy of Balaam in Num. 24:17, "a star shall come forth out of Jacob, and a sceptre shall rise out of Israel." Among the Dead Sea Scrolls there is a fragment from Cave 4 (cited as 4Q175), which is a collection of proof texts in which this Balaam oracle is combined with the prophecy of a prophet like Moses (Deut. 18:18-19). This shows that speculation on the star was current in the 1st century B.C. or A.D.

Since the birth of John the Baptist was announced in the time of Herod (Luke 1:5), Luke, like Matthew, probably dated Jesus' birth during the king's reign. But Herod died in 4 B.C., and thus the Christian era, calculated only in the 7th century, forces Jesus' birth to be dated B.C.

Only a late tradition makes the magi into "three kings" and gives them names. Their royal character must have been suggested by Ps. 72:10 and Isa. 60:6 ("gold and frankincense").

The grisly story that Herod had all the boy babies two years old and younger massacred (Matt. 2:16-18) is not supported by any independent evidence, but it corresponds to the character of the king. He had an insane fear of any threat to his life or his power, and when his favorite wife Mariamne was accused of plotting against him, he had her executed. Herod had eight wives and children by most of them. There were continual intrigues in the court in which his brother and sister were sometimes involved; and late in his reign he had his two sons by Mariamne and another son put to death.

As Matthew tells it, Herod's plot against the infant Jesus was foiled because Joseph was warned in a dream to take the Holy Family to Egypt (Matt. 2:13-15). This would have been a hard journey. One can only guess at possible routes, but assuming that it is at least 125 miles from Bethlehem to Nazareth, the distance from Bethlehem to the northern border of Egypt would have been only a little less.

Matthew wrote the entire infancy narrative in such a way as to bring out parallels between events in the Old Testament and in the life of Jesus. Joseph the husband of Mary corresponds to Joseph the son of Jacob who was sold into Egypt, who had dreams and could interpret dreams. The star in the east recalls Balaam's prophecy of the star. The evangelist connects the murder of the innocents with a passage in Jer. 31:15 in which Rachel, the ancestress of the northern tribes, weeps over the deportation of Israelites to Assyria.

Not far from Manger Square in Bethlehem is the chapel of the Milk Grotto where the family was believed to have stayed and Mary nursed the child, just before the flight into Egypt.

The Holy Family duplicates the wanderings of the children of Israel. Joseph, again instructed by a dream, takes his wife and child into the Promised Land (Matt. 2:19-23). But, just as the Israelites could not enter Canaan at once but had to travel east of the Jordan valley, so this family was afraid of Herod's son Archelaus and had to approach Galilee by the way of Transjordan. Matthew's account ends with them settling in Nazareth, and this also, the evangelist believed, was in accordance with prophecy. It is not certain what passage he had in mind. Samson had been destined to be a Nazirite (Judg. 13:3, 7); but possibly the reference is to a passage in Isa. 11:1 in which the word translated "branch" has the consonants *nṣr*. This predicts the Messiah:

> There shall come forth a shoot from the stump of Jesse,
> and a branch shall grow out of his roots (RSV).

2

Nazareth In Galilee

I

In the Gospel of John, Jesus says of Nathanael, "Here is really an Israelite in whom there is no guile." Yet a little before this, when the same man heard of Jesus, he asked, "Can anything good come out of Nazareth?" (John 1:46). Much later, in Jerusalem, the people debated whether Jesus could possibly be the Messiah. Someone said, "Surely the Messiah does not come from Galilee; doesn't the Scripture say that it is from the seed of David and from Bethlehem, the village where David was, that the Messiah comes?" (7:42). Nazareth was a very obscure place.

There was a time, indeed, when skeptical historians doubted that Nazareth existed at all in Jesus' time. The town was known only from Christian sources, not Jewish. It is only in the 3rd century A.D. that a man named Conon, who was martyred in Asia Minor in the persecution under the emperor Decius (249-251), claimed to be from Nazareth and a member of Christ's family.

It was also argued that the epithet *Nazoraios* originally meant "one who is religiously observant," or that it came from a prophecy in the Old Testament promising a Messiah from the branch or shoot of David. A further puzzle was that these words contained a Semitic consonant *ş* while the Greek words always used *z*.

All this reasoning, which once seemed plausible, has now been exploded. Many years ago the great archaeologist and Semitist William F. Albright showed that a Hebrew *ṣ* could be transliterated into Greek as *z*. More recently, a Hebrew inscription from Caesarea on the seacoast gives a list of priests from several towns. Some were from the course of priests called Happizzez (2 Chron. 24:3-15) who lived in Naṣerath. So the village actually existed in Jesus' day and it had the name that Albright had conjectured.

Nazareth continued to be obscure until the time of Constantine. Epiphanius, bishop of Salamis in Cyprus, remarked that in this period only Jews lived there. Christians came later. The indefatigable traveller Egeria was shown a cave in Nazareth where it was believed that Mary had lived. Evidently a basilica was built over this house in the 6th century. Then in 670 another pilgrim named Arculf saw two churches, one in the centre of the city over the house where Jesus had been brought up, and another on the site of the house where Gabriel announced his birth.

These churches were mostly destroyed about 700 when Muslim Arabs invaded the land. In the Crusader period, when Tancred was prince of Galilee, the churches were rebuilt. After this there was another destruction. The resurgence of Nazareth begins in 1620, the year in which the pilgrims landed in New England. The Franciscans were now recognized as official guardians of the holy places in Palestine and were able to purchase the ruins where the present Church of the Annunciation stands.

II

Jesus certainly grew to manhood in Nazareth. After his baptism and temptation he began his ministry in Galilee (Mark 1:14). He may have returned briefly to his home town, but his actual work began in or near Capernaum, where he settled (Matt. 4:13; Mark 1:21; Luke 4:23).

Matthew understands this as fulfilment of a poetic prophecy:

> Land of Zebulun and land of Naphtali,
>> the way of the Sea, the other side of Jordan,
>>> Galilee of the nations!
> The people who sat in darkness
>> saw a great light,
> and for those who were seated in the place and
>> shadow of death
>>> light has sprung up (Matt. 4:15-16; Isa. 9:1-2).

Galilee was the territory traditionally assigned to these two tribes (Josh. 19:10-16, 32-39). Naphtali extends along the Sea of Galilee and stretches northward as far as Lake Huleh, which has now been drained by the Israelis. Zebulun is to the south and west. The west and north borders cannot be defined exactly, but Galilee did not include the Phoenician coastal plain or Dan and Caesarea Philippi. Nazareth lies at the extreme south edge of the latter region in a valley opening out to a cliff. Below this cliff is the plain of Esdraelon.

Galil means circle or region, and in the days of the Hebrew monarchy it was known as Galilee of the nations (or Gentiles). It was only during the Maccabaean monarchy that Jews settled here in any numbers.

The region is divided into two parts, approximately by the plain of Rameh, on a line drawn from Capernaum west toward Akko or Ptolemais, north of Haifa. Upper Galilee is mountainous, much of it from 1,500 to 3,900 feet in elevation. It was very sparsely settled, but from the 2nd century on many Jews moved in, and there are ruins of synagogues at Mount Meiron and in its environs. In contrast, Lower Galilee was thickly populated, and although the historian Josephus exaggerates, he says that every part of the soil was cultivated. The altitude varies from 696 feet below sea level at the sea of Galilee to about 500 feet above, except for mountains to the southeast, Tabor being the highest. The bedrock is mostly limestone, with the exception that the eastern part of Galilee was at one time volcanic. There are hot springs south of

Tiberias, and much of this portion is covered by basalt rock. This has formed fertile alluvial soil in places like the plain of Gennesaret, which Josephus called "the ambition of nature." Where limestone is present it has created the reddish *terra rossa* and Mediterranean brown which are found in many parts of Palestine. The rainfall varies with the elevation for example from 16.37 inches annually on the shore of the lake to 25 inches at Nazareth.

In Galilee it is rather easy to observe the different kinds of soil mentioned by Jesus in the parable of the Sower (Mark 4:1-9): paths trodden through a field where the birds devour the seed, a thin covering of earth over a rocky ledge, clumps of thorns, and the good earth of Gennesaret which can yield a hundred times the sowing.

We have been describing a rather small territory. Galilee under Roman administration was about 35 by 25 miles in extent. Reno County in Kansas would be approximately this size. Galilee is a little larger than Wiltshire in England or the Grand Duchy of Luxembourg.

III

The ambition of the Maccabaean kings was to make their realm as great as the kingdom of David and Solomon. Jews may have moved into Galilee as early as the time of Aristobulus I (104-103 B.C.), but it was his brother Alexander Jannaeus (103-76) who conquered Galilee and did his best to make it Jewish. Yet in Jesus' time the region was a mosaic, with pagan and Jewish settlements here and there.

For example, Sepphoris, about five miles north of Nazareth, was largely a pagan city. After the death of Herod the Great there were uprisings here, and the Roman general Varus burnt the city and made slaves of many of its people. The emperor Augustus honored Herod's will by assigning Galilee and Peraea (Transjordan) to his son Herod Antipas as tetrarch ("ruler of one-fourth"). Antipas soon rebuilt Sepphoris, gave it the name "Imperial," and made it his capital. It continued to be the seat of government until A.D. 25, when he moved it to Tiberias.

After the first Jewish revolt (A.D. 66-73), Galilee became one of the most important centres of Judaism. In the 2nd century there was a rabbinical academy at Sepphoris, and Judah ha-Nasi, who compiled the Mishnah, the first part of the Talmud, lived there.

But during the lifetime of Jesus the city must have been pagan. It is strange that he is quoted as telling his disciples, "Do not go on any road of the Gentiles and do not enter a town of the Samaritans (Matt. 10:5), because this seems contrary to his own actions. If he spoke these words, it may have been only an extreme way of insisting that the mission of the disciples must be to "the lost sheep of the house of Israel" (10:6). Jesus could scarcely have avoided walking on roads travelled by pagans.

IV

In turbulent days immediately after Herod the Great, there were serious revolts in Judaea as well as at Sepphoris. The Roman general Varus crucified 2,000 Jews in and near Jerusalem. But the Galileans had an especial reputation for fierce independence. In A.D. 6, a man known as Judas the Galilean or the Gaulonite, who evidently came from the Golan Heights, led an armed revolt. If we may suppose that Jesus was born about 6 B.C., he would have been twelve years old at this time. The occasion for the uprising was a census ordered by Quirinius, the legate of Syria. Archelaus had just been removed as ethnarch of Judaea and that province was made an integral part of the empire to be ruled by prefects.

Josephus says,

> Within this limited area, and although surrounded by such powerful foreign nations, the two Galilees have always resisted any hostile invasion, for their inhabitants are from infancy inured to war, and have at all times been numerous; never did the men lack courage nor the country men (*Jewish War* iii. 3. 2, Thackeray's tr.)

Galilee was in fact strategic. Roads led from Egypt through the coastal plain to Ptolemais and from there to the Sea of Galilee, then north toward Damascus and the north and east. It was in Galilee that Herod the Great defeated the Parthians in 39-38 B.C. in order to establish his rule. The first Jewish revolt broke out in A.D. 66 and the general Cestius Gallus sent the Twelfth Legion to Galilee in an attempt to put it down. Toward the end of that year, Josephus organized an army and a civil administration for Galilee. Vespasian took command in the winter of 66/67. When he besieged Jotapata north of Sepphoris, Josephus and forty men took refuge in a cave, and now follows one of the great stories of all time. Out of desperation, the men decided to die so that they might not fall into the hands of the Romans. Lots were cast to see who was next to be slain, and at last there were two survivors. Josephus was one of the two, and he persuaded the other to desert with him to the Romans. He tells us that he believed submission was the only hope for survival of his people. Brought before Vespasian, he predicted that the general would become emperor, and this in fact happened. A little later he was proclaimed by his army. It was only after other victories in Galilee, at Gischala and Taricheae near Tiberias, that Vespasian was able to march on Jerusalem.

The Galilean Jews of the 1st century seem also to have been independent and recalcitrant in religious matters. The Pharisees of Jerusalem, who were townspeople and belonged economically to what we would call the middle class, had a poor opinion of the Galileans. They regarded them as ignorant country boors, careless of the law. There was a question whether they regularly paid tithes on olive oil that they sold. Probably many of the men stigmatized by the rabbis as *'amme ha-aretz* ("people of the land") were from Galilee. A remark attributed to the Pharisees, "These people who do not know the law are accursed" (John 7:49) expresses this attitude. One famous rabbi said, "No *'am ha-aretz* is religious."

These political struggles and religious controversies partly determined the mental climate in which Jesus was born and grew up, and his message of the Reign of God must be considered against this background.

V

Luke says that Jesus' birth was announced in Nazareth. Perhaps Matthew did not know this tradition, for he first mentions Nazareth when the Holy Family returns from Egypt, but all the gospels agree that as a young man Jesus lived there. The tradition in the Gospel of John does not even connect him with Bethlehem.

There are apocryphal gospels which tell of Jesus' childhood and relate fantastic miracles that he was supposed to have performed. These stories can be ignored as pious fancies. Nothing is known of the "hidden years" except for one charming and lifelike story in the Gospel of Luke. The family had visited Jerusalem for Passover. Jesus got separated from the company and was finally found in the Temple area engaged in discussion with the teachers there and asking them questions (2:41-52). At the age of twelve he was ready to take a man's place in synagogue worship, just as Jewish boys have done for centuries when they become *bar mitzvah* ("son of the commandment").

Jesus' first religious education would have been in the home. It is the prerogative of a Jewish mother to light the sabbath candles; and in many other ways, by word and example, she teaches her children. He may well have attended a synagogue school where he learned to read the Scriptures, many parts of which he knew by heart. He never seems to have been the disciple of a rabbi, but when he was a boy he amazed the experts by his understanding and answers.

Much of Jesus' education was practical. Mark calls him a *tekton*, Matthew the son of the *tekton*. This word can mean "carpenter" or more generally "builder." (An *architekton* was originally a master builder.) So perhaps Jesus could work with stone and mud brick. An early tradition says that Joseph made ox-yokes and plows.

VI

At some point in his early ministry Jesus experienced rejection in his home village. The gospels do not fix the time precisely. Mark 6:1-6 records the event only after Jesus has been very active and has met significant success and opposition, while in Luke it occurs near the beginning (Luke 4:16-30). Even here the story implies that he has already performed miracles in Capernaum (4:23), and one must realize that the authors of the gospels locate scenes they best fit a theological purpose. Luke wishes to show that at the very start of his ministry Jesus was spurned by his own people.

Both stories agree that the villagers wished to cut him down to their own size. After all, he was only a home town boy. In fact, says Luke, they were so offended that they rushed him out of the town, intending to cast him down from the cliff, but he escaped from them. We do not know that he ever returned to Nazareth, unless John thinks that it was there that his brothers urged him to go to Judaea (John 7:3-5).

VII

Nazareth is the largest Christian city in the Holy Land. Of its present population of about 35,000, perhaps two-thirds are Christians. The principal streets may seem rather miscellaneous, as in many Arab towns which contain 19th and 20th century structures, but in the older parts of Nazareth there are streets and markets that are old-fashioned and oriental.

The Arab Christian population is a religious mosaic, as it is everywhere in the Holy Land. First, there are several Catholic churches with organizations independent of one another but under allegiance to the Pope. The Latin Catholics owe their strength principally to the work of the Franciscans for the past 350 years or more. Several other religious orders operate schools, hospitals, orphanages and other social agencies. The Greek Catholics, sometimes called

Nazareth; Plain of Esdraelon in background

Melkites, have a liturgy and customs much like those of the
Greek Orthodox. They have an archbishop and a seminary
in Nazareth, churches, a convent and schools. In fact, there
at least 25 villages in Galilee that are predominantly Christian. Most of these people belong to the Greek Catholic
community, others to the Latin, Anglican and Protestant
denominations. Many new churches and other institutions
have been built in recent years. Another Catholic community,
the Maronites, whose centre is in Lebanon, have a church in
Nazareth.

The Orthodox Church, which is in communion with the Ecumenical Patriarch in Istanbul, claims to be the oldest in the Holy Land. The Greek Orthodox are represented in Nazareth by the old church of St. Gabriel and its congregation. The Russian Orthodox also have a house of prayer in the city.

There is also a Coptic church in Nazareth. The Copts are the ancient Christians of Egypt. They are not in communion with the Greek Orthodox because they do not accept the decrees of the Council of Chalcedon (A.D. 451) but in other respects they are very similar to them.

For many years there has been a church of the Episcopal Evangelical community (Anglican) in Nazareth. The Church of Scotland (Presbyterian) maintains a hospital and training school for Arab nurses. Other denominations have churches here, Baptists, Nazarene and Church of Christ, and the YMCA has a hospice, youth centre and hostel.

VIII

The Church of the Annunciation is in the centre of the city and visible from all directions. The Franciscans built a church here in 1730, and this was demolished in 1955 to make way for the brilliant modern structure which was completed in 1969. The architects designed it so that one can see remains of a 12th century Crusader church and also one of the apses of an older Byzantine one. Here there is a basin that is believed to be a baptistery dating from before the time of Constantine. Steps lead down to a mosaic floor bearing the inscription "Gift of Conon, deacon of Jerusalem."

This cave may be the one which Egeria visited in 384 and was said to be the house of Mary.

Another very interesting place connected with the Annunciation story is the Greek Orthodox Church of St. Gabriel on the north side of the city. It is located near a famous spring, and water bubbles up in a basin in the apse of the church. The spring itself is perhaps 55 feet away inside the hill, and it also feeds the "Virgin's Fountain" located north-east of St. Gabriel's.

The tradition of this spring goes back to an apocryphal gospel known as the Protevangelium of James. This was written in the 3rd century or possibly even in the late 2nd. Part of it reads as follows:

> And Mary took the pitcher and went forth to draw water. Just then a voice said, "Hail, you who are highly favored among women." And she looked to the right and the left to see whence the voice came. Trembling, she went to the house, put down the pitcher, took the purple cloth, sat down, and drew out the thread. Now an angel of the Lord suddenly stood before her and said, "Do not fear, Mary, for you have found favor before the Lord of all and you shall conceive from his Word."

Arculf is the first pilgrim to mention a church built on this site; he saw it in 670. Later in the middle ages it was modified into a circular style. Such places of worship, like Constantine's original basilica in Bethlehem, were designed to display holy places. The present Greek church replaces the mediaeval structure.

North of the Church of the Annunciation is the Church of St. Joseph, constructed in 1914. There was evidently a mediaeval church with three apses here. Steps lead down to a basin which is somewhat like the baptistery of the Annunciation. Beneath the basin other steps lead down to an underground cave. Since the 17th century this has been identified as Joseph's workshop, but there is no basis for this tradition.

Nor is there any firm foundation for the belief that the Synagogue Church (Greek Catholic) marks the spot where Jesus preached on the text from Isaiah. It is, however, a very interesting building. The Piacenza pilgrim in 570 was shown what was claimed to be the synagogue, and in the 13th century there is a tradition that this had been remodelled into a church, but the location of this is actually unknown.

Finally, Christians were certain to worship at the place where the angry citizens of Nazareth intended to cast Jesus down into the valley. The cliff fits the notice in Luke 4:29. The Maronite Church of the Precipitation is nearby.

3

To the Sea of Galilee

I

About four miles northeast of Nazareth is a village named Cana which late tradition claims to be the place where Jesus attended a wedding and turned water into wine (John 2:1-12). It is a convenient place for pious pilgrimage. A Greek Orthodox church was built there in 1566. There are also a Franciscan church, constructed in 1880, and a Greek Catholic church.

The Arabic name of the town is Kefr Kenna (*Kefr* means "village"). Arabic place names often preserve old traditions, but the doubling of the consonant *n* raises a problem. Another site, about nine miles north of Nazareth, has a better claim to be ancient Cana. This is Khirbet (ruin of) Qana, and in Arabic it is also known as Qana el-Jalil, Cana of Galilee (John 2:1). Its disadvantage is that it is off the road and hard to reach. Here there are only some ruins that have not yet been excavated.

Qana ought to mean something like "place of reeds," and below the ruins there is a marshy plain in which reeds still grow. Josephus says that he once lived in this place, and St. Jerome in the 4th century gives Cana a location that fits the ruin fairly well. The place was also identified by pilgrims in the 12th century.

As one comes nearer Tiberias, still in the higher country, the Horns of Hattin are visible to the north. These are peaks of basalt rock. Here Saladin fought the decisive battle against the Crusaders on July 4, 1187. By confronting Saladin, Guy de Lusignan, king of Jerusalem, hoped to relieve pressure on Tiberias. The Crusader governor of Tiberias warned against this as a foolish effort, but Guy gave in to pressure from the Grand Master of the Templars, and the result was a slaughter. After this disaster, a few places like St. Jean d'Acre (Akko) held out for a time, but this was the end of the Frankish kingdom of Jerusalem.

Beyond this the road descends steeply to Tiberias and the Sea of Galilee.

II

This lake is part of one of the geological wonders of the earth. It is in the great rift which begins in the Beqa' valley of Lebanon south of the Amanus mountains, and extends through the Jordan valley and Dead Sea, the Red Sea, and in Africa as far as Lake Victoria Nyanza. This explains why vegetation found in the Jordan valley is similar to that in the Sudan. The surface of the Sea of Galilee is 696 feet below the level of the Mediterranean.

We call it a sea only because of the English versions of the Bible; its waters are, however, moderately saline. The earliest name for it was Chinnereth. *Kinnor* means "lyre" or "harp," but it is hard to understand how ancient Hebrews could have thought it was shaped like such an instrument. Later it was called Gennesar or Gennesaret (1 Macc. 11:67; Luke 5:1) and still later the Sea of Tiberias (John 6:1; 21:1). The lake is 13 miles in length, and eight miles broad, east to west, at its widest point. The greatest depth is about 200 feet.

There is a good view of it from above Tiberias. I remember seeing a spectacular sunrise over it when I was in an Italian hospice in Tiberias, and from the traditional Mount of the Beatitudes there is a splendid prospect. Like all such bodies of water its color seems to change, green and blue and sometimes almost white.

The climate is sub-tropical and bananas and date palms grow on the shores. At the south end the waters flow into the Jordan river. There is a place on the west side of the lake where the mountains form a natural theatre. Some years ago an experiment was tried in one of these coves, and it was found that voices from a boat could be heard distinctly on the shore. This illustrates Mark's introduction to the parable of the Sower (4:1): "Again he began to teach beside the sea, and a great crowd gathered to him, so he got in a boat and was seated in the sea; and all the crowd was on the land facing the sea."

The north shore is very shallow. Behind it are several marshes and lagoons where papyrus and other plants grow. Here and there are patches of dry land now cultivated by the Israelis, and wheat can be harvested there as early as April.

III

One who comes to the Sea of Galilee for the first time may expect it to evoke the presence of Jesus and to encourage prayer. How people respond to holy places depends much on their previous religious experience. Whittier, the "good gray" Quaker poet, expressed a familiar sentiment:

> O Sabbath rest in Galilee,
>   O calm of hills above,
> Where Jesus knelt to share with thee
> The silence of eternity
>   Interpreted by love.

The shore is a busy place. Tourists and pilgrims throng the Jewish and Christian holy places, and pleasure boats ply back and forth between Tiberias and Ein Gev on the east side. In the 19th and early 20th centuries there were fewer people here, and it is interesting to read the accounts of travellers. Ernest Renan was a French priest who became a free-thinker and left the church. After making a sentimental journey to the Holy Land he wrote a *Life of Jesus* which portrayed him as a benevolent mystic, in other words Renan's own ideal. The Holy Land was portrayed as a realm of peace and beauty. The New York preacher, Henry Van Dyke, whose hymn of joy set to Beethoven's music is in most hymnals, found the open country more to his taste than the ancient churches. His book, *Out of Doors in the Holy Land*, is still worth reading.

Mark Twain travelled here from Damascus in a camping caravan with the greatest luxury then possible. He remembered the gospel story with reverence, but found the local Jews and Arabs dirty and unattractive. At that time Capernaum was only a "shapeless ruin," and he described Magdala and Tiberias as stinking and squalid. Mark considered Lake Tahoe much more beautiful than the Sea of Galilee, and in *The Innocents Abroad* he wrote: "If all the poetry and nonsense that have been discharged upon the fountains and bland scenery of this region were collected in a book, it would make a most valuable volume to burn."

In the time of Jesus, Galilee was neither the ideal region of the poets nor the place seen by Mark Twain that had been misruled and neglected by the Turkish empire for centuries. It was certainly not quiet. Along the west shore ran an important highway of commerce. Agriculture flourished. Armies often passed this way. The gospels record Jesus escaping to the hill country or some other deserted place for prayer, and even so, people who were in need sought him out.

The Holy Land is secularized to a great degree—what other sacred place is not?—and not all its inhabitants practice their ancestral religions, yet many Muslims retire to their clean, spacious and quiet mosques for prayer, Jews go to synagogues, and Arab Christians can be found at their devotions in the great churches of Jerusalem and Bethlehem and the smaller shrines in Galilee. In 1947 I remember visiting Tell en-Nasbeh, an archaeological site a few miles north of Jerusalem and just south of Ramallah. Across the road at a place called Maloufiyeh there was at that time a small factory where arak, the local liquor, was distilled. We came across a young man who worked for the British mandatory government overseeing the collection of taxes on arak. He said that he had just been on top of the tell reading the Sermon on the Mount in his Arabic Bible.

It is always possible to find God, or rather to be found by him, at home, in familiar surroundings, and also at the Sea of Galilee if one takes the time to recollect his presence. The sites one visits along the lake may help; or it may be enough to sit quietly in some place like the traditional Mount of the Beatitudes and look at the Sea of Galilee through the palm trees.

4

Tiberias

I

Tiberias is now a modern Jewish city, much favored as a vacation resort, with good hotels, more modest hospices, and many restaurants which serve "St. Peter's fish," *Tilapia galilaea*. One can take a boat ride to Ein Gev on the east side of the lake or enjoy the hot baths just south of the town. Many of the older buildings are constructed from the black basalt rock found in the neighborhood.

The population is predominantly Jewish, but a few Christian and Muslim Arabs live in the city.

Herod Antipas moved his capital from Sepphoris to Tiberias about A.D. 25. This man was the son of Herod the Great and his wife Malthace. The emperor Augustus had not granted him the title of king but only that of tetrarch, but he ruled Galilee and Peraea (Transjordan) as a client prince of the empire. He named the city for Tiberius, who was the emperor then and throughout Jesus' ministry. Antipas' father had been a great builder, and the son made this new city as magnificent as he could, with a stadium, a palace, and a large synagogue.

There was an ancient cemetery on the site, and the stricter Jews at this time avoided it. But not all Galilean Jews were so scrupulous, and these included especially Antipas' courtiers and friends. Probably both Jews and pagans inhabited the town. Later, at the time of the first Jewish revolt, Tiberias did not resist Vespasian's army.

The gospels do not mention this city as such, except in one passage, when after the feeding of the Five Thousand, some boats from Tiberias come to the place of the miracle and then go on to Capernaum (John 6:23). But Herod Antipas figures several times in the gospel story. At the instigation of his wife Herodias he has John the Baptist beheaded (Mark 6:17-29), and when he hears of Jesus' activities he says superstitiously that he is John the Baptist risen from the dead (Mark 6:14-16). As Jesus is about to leave Galilee for Jerusalem, some Pharisees who are evidently friendly to him warn that Herod intends to kill him (Luke 13:31-33)—and Jesus refers to the prince as "that fox." Among the women who followed Jesus on this last journey was Joanna, the wife of Chuza, Herod's *epitropos*. This word is often translated "steward," but it can also mean a government official. It would seem that Jesus' activity in Galilee was noticed in high circles of society, both favorably and unfavorably.

Luke portrays Herod Antipas as a man of great curiosity. It is only in his gospel that at the time of the trial Pilate sends Jesus to Herod. The Galilean ruler evidently considered Jesus a harmless person of no importance (Luke 23:6-12, 15).

II

Jewish scholars learned in Torah began to leave Jerusalem and Judaea after the destruction of the Temple in A.D. 70. The first centre of rabbinic study may have been at Jamnia (Jabneh) on the coastal plain. After the second revolt (A.D. 132-135) the emperor Hadrian renamed Jerusalem as Aelia Capitolina and made it a pagan city. We hear now of an academy at Sepphoris where Judah ha-Nasi taught. About 220, one of R. Judah's last disciples, R. Joḥanan ben Nappaha, founded a rabbinical school at Tiberias. Scruples about the uncleanness of that city now disappeared, and the Talmud contains legends of how the city was purified. For centuries, along with Babylonia, Galilee was the great centre of study of the Torah. The Mishnah already existed, and the remaining part of the Jerusalem Talmud (the Gemara) had its beginnings here. Tiberias came to be known as one of the four holy cities of Palestine.

Famous rabbis are buried there: in an enclosure near the Public Garden are the tombs of Joḥanan ben Zakkai (1st century), Eliezer ben Hyrcanus (2nd century) and Moses Maimonides (12th century). On a hillside above is the tomb of Aqiba (2nd century).

A visit to Tiberias can be the occasion for Christian pilgrims to gain a better understanding of Judaism, the religion in which Jesus and Paul were brought up. The attempt of Roman emperors to stamp out Judaism failed. What the great Pharisaic scholars did was to turn away from involvement in politics and to try to instruct all Jewish people in observance of the law. The new Christian Church now confronted a revived and vigorous Judaism and generally considered it a threat. The hostility between the two communities is reflected in the one-sided condemnation of Pharisaism that one finds especially in the gospels of Matthew and John, and in the curse on heretics that at about this time was inserted into the Eighteen Benedictions of the synagogue liturgy but was later removed. Although Christians and Jews are often in disagreement today, the traditions of Tiberias permit a Christian to see aspects of Judaism that he or she might otherwise miss. There are fundamental differences between the two religions but also misunderstandings on both sides. Both of course accept the Hebrew Scriptures, and it is fair to say that modern study of Judaism enriches understanding of Jesus and Paul.

The tombs of famous rabbis at Tiberias are symbols of this. There is, for example, a beautiful story about R. Joḥanan ben Zakkai, who is buried here. After the destruction of the Temple he and one of his friends stood looking at the ruins. "Alas for us," said the companion, "for the place where the sins of Israel were atoned for is no more." "Do not grieve," Joḥanan answered, "for we have what is better than sacrifice, as it is written, 'I desire mercy and not sacrifice'"(Hos. 6:6; Matt. 12:6-7). It was this rabbi, who, more than any other single person, made the survival and consolidation of the Jewish tradition possible.

The tractate Aboth in the Mishnah contains several of his sayings. One of these expresses his piety: "If you have accomplished much in the law do not claim credit for yourself, because it was to this end that you were created." Another tradition here mentions his five chief disciples, and one of these is Eliezer ben Hyrcanus, who is buried near him. This saying compares two disciples, one of whom is a perfect learner and the other a creative spirit. "Eliezer ben Hyrcanus is a plastered cistern which loses not a drop . . . Eliezer ben Arak is an ever-flowing spring."

Another of these saints, Moses Maimonides, is notable because he expressed Jewish theology in terms of Aristotle's philosophy, as St. Thomas Aquinas was later to do with Christian theology. Then there is R. Aqiba, buried on the hillside. At the time of the second Jewish revolt he acclaimed the revolutionary prince Simeon bar Koziba as the Messiah. This man was also known as bar Kokhba ("son of the star," a possible reference to Balaam's prophecy in Num. 24:17). Simeon's revolt was a hopeless attempt to restore independence to the Jewish people of Palestine, but he ruled the land for a time and coined money as a sign of sovereignty. One can only admire Aqiba's faith and patriotism. The Romans put him to death, and when he went to execution we are told that he "took the yoke of the law" upon himself by repeating the words of the Shema' which orthodox Jews recite twice daily, "Hear, O Israel, the Lord is One."

III

The hot springs just south of Tiberias must have been used for healing even in pagan days. Certainly by the 1st century A.D. they were put to good use. All through the empire, from Ancyra (Ankara) to Bath in England, the Romans constructed elaborate baths, and Herod Antipas and his courtiers must have enjoyed such luxuries here.

Archaeologists have uncovered fine mosaic floors, and one mosaic that portrays the zodiac is influenced by classical style. There are several mosaic inscriptions in Greek, and one in Aramaic.

5

The West Shore

I. Magdala

Pilgrims are not likely to stop at the site of Magdala because little is to be seen there. As one goes northward along the lake it is about three miles from Tiberias. Yet it was very important in New Testament times. The place was evidently called *Migdal*, which means "tower," probably because at one time there was a fortress here. It is also at the junction of the lake road with a highway that came down from the hills. In Jesus' day it was a flourishing city and a centre of the fishing industry. Josephus mentions its Greek name Taricheae, which means a factory for salting and pickling fish (*Jewish War* ii. 21. 8; iii. 9.7—10.5). Fish preserved by these methods were exported from here to Jerusalem and Damascus and even as far as Spain.

The interest of Magdala for Christians is that it was evidently the home of Mary Magdalene. Tradition has given a distorted picture of this lady as the prototype of penitent sinners. The name of Magdalen College at Oxford is pronounced "maudlin," and the adjective that is spelled in the latter way has come to refer to extravagant emotion. This fact of language arises because from early times Mary was identified as the sinful woman who wept on Jesus' feet and anointed them (Luke 7:36-50), probably because Mary is mentioned just afterward. She was also confused with Mary of Bethany (Luke 10:38-42), perhaps because Luke's stories were combined with John 11:2 and Mark 14:3-9.

But what Luke actually tells us about Mary Magdalene is that she was one of the women who accompanied Jesus as he went about proclaiming the Kingdom of God and that "seven demons had gone out of her" (Luke 8:2). Mark's tradition is that she was one of a similar company of women who followed Jesus from Galilee and watched the Crucifixion from a distance (Mark 15:40-41; cf. Luke 23:49). Mary Magdalene was with Mary of Joses when they saw where Jesus was buried (Mark 15:47), and she, Mary of James and Salome came to the tomb and received the first message of the Resurrection (Mark 16:1-8).

Although according to Mark the women were afraid to tell anyone the news, Luke says that they reported it to the eleven disciples, and he substitutes the name of Joanna for Salome (Luke 24:9-10). We are evidently dealing with various traditions; thus in Matt. 28:9-10, Jesus meets the women, and in John 20:11-18, Mary Magdalene is the first to see the risen Lord.

In all these traditions she is a central and heroic figure. The only note about Mary Magdalene that might be thought negative is that she had suffered from seven demons—physical or nervous maladies. The biblical writers lived in a male-oriented culture, but they preserved the memory that Jesus had women disciples who were at times more devoted and courageous than the men. Why were they not present at the Last Supper? Were they in the kitchen?

Later tradition had to invent a sequel to the story of this Mary. An early legend in the eastern Church says that she went with the apostle John to Ephesus and died there. The west had a different tradition, first known in the 9th century: with Martha and Lazarus she came to the south of France, and her tomb was near Aix-en-Provence. A variant of this is told at les Saintes Maries at the mouth of the Rhone river. The three Maries, Magdalene, Mary of James and the mother of Jesus, arrived here by ship, together with their black servant Sarah, who is especially venerated by gypsy pilgrims every year.

Fishermen on the Sea of Galilee

II. Fishing

Mark does not tell us where Jesus met his first four disciples. It may have been at Magdala or anywhere along the shore. He has just said that Jesus came into Galilee proclaiming the Good News of the coming Reign of God. As throughout the gospel, we have a series of loosely connected episodes. Then he goes on:

> Passing along beside the Sea of Galilee he saw Simon and
> Andrew, Simon's brother, casting a net into the sea; for

they were fishermen. Jesus said to them, "Come after me and I will make you fishers of human beings." They immediately left their nets behind and followed him. And as he went on a little way farther he saw James the son of Zebedee and John his brother. They were in the boat mending their nets. He immediately summoned them; and they left their father Zebedee in the boat with the hired men and went off after him (Mark 1:16-20).

Fishing is mentioned several times in the gospels. Luke has a different story of the enlistment of disciples which curiously does not mention Andrew. Simon has been unlucky fishing all night, but in obedience to Jesus' word he launches out into deep water, lowers the nets, and hauls in a great catch of fish (Luke 5:1-11). This may have been originally a resurrection story transferred to this place, for a similar and very beautiful account of fishing is told of the risen Christ in John 21:1-14. The Lord has kindled a fire on the beach and, after their amazing catch, provides them with the bread and fish which came to be symbols of the Eucharist.

The gospels mention two kinds of nets, both of which have been used in the Sea of Galilee in recent times.

Peter and Andrew used a circular net, with weights and a draw rope around the circumference. Once dropped in the lake, the rope can be pulled tight so as to "enclose" the fish (Luke 5:6). The other type is a seine, a long rectangle that can be worked by two boats as they draw the fish toward the shore. In the parable of Matt. 13:47-50 the men sort the fish, save the good ones and reject the bad. The gospel uses this as a parable of the last judgment.

"Fishing for human beings" is always an ominous metaphor in the Old Testament. The Chaldaean conqueror who menaces Israel brings men up "with a hook, he drags them out with his net, he gathers them in his seine" (Hab. 1:15), and in Jeremiah's prophecy (16:16) the Lord himself threatens that he will send many fishers who will catch idolaters.

Jesus turns this figure of speech in the opposite direction. His disciples are to fish for human beings to give them life, not death.

About forty years ago a book called the Gospel of Thomas was discovered in Egypt. It is one item in a whole library of books written in Coptic on papyrus. These belonged to Gnostics, a sectarian group that most of the Christian Church rejected as holding strange and erroneous doctrines. The Gospel of Thomas is a collection of sayings attributed to Jesus. Many of these are tinged with Gnosticism, but others reflect a tradition as old as any of the canonical gospels, and scholars take them seriously. Several parables are included, and one tells how a wise fisherman caught many fish. Most of these were too small to be of any use, but he found one large fish and kept it. This reminds us of another of Jesus' parables. A merchant in search of splendid pearls found one that was exceedingly precious, and he went and sold everything he had and bought that pearl (Matt. 13:45-46). The disciples did something like that when they gave up the advantages of their previous lives, accepted Jesus' message of the Kingdom of God, and followed him. Simon Peter, Andrew, James and John were among these. Mary Magdalene was another.

III. The Church of the Loaves and Fishes

Just north of Magdala we come to the little plain of Gennesaret, which deserves the extravagant praise of its fertility expressed by Josephus. The need of modern Israel to survive has led its people to make full use of what such soil provides.

Still farther north, a little south of Capernaum, is a place anciently known by a Greek name, Heptapegon, "seven springs." In Arabic speech this has been modified to eṭ-Ṭabgha. Here lies one of the great archaeological and artistic treasures of the Holy Land. In 1982, mostly with the help of funds from Germany, the Benedictines completed and dedicated a church which preserves and displays the mosaic floors of a 5th century church. It is in the Byzantine style of that early period. There was in fact an earlier church of about A.D. 350.

When that indefatigable nun Egeria passed this way some time in the years 381-384 she saw palm trees and the seven springs, and she said that this was the field where the Lord fed the people.

Et-Ṭabgha leads one to reflect on how nearly all people use their artistic gifts to celebrate religious sentiments. In primitive societies religion, art and daily life are not separate enterprises; they are all integrated in a single culture. Modern people cut life up into several compartments, yet they still express religious impulses in artistic forms.

The ancient Hebrews and Jews had the Sinai tradition of the Ten Commandments, which taught that one must not make a graven image of God. When Herod's Temple was built, the rabbis saw to it that this was observed strictly. Faith must express itself, and the writers of the Old Testament pictured God in words. The prophets and psalmists were poets. So was Jesus.

The Israelites could, however, construct places for meeting God's presence. Solomon's Temple was not large by our standards, but it was made as sumptuous as possible. After the exile it was replaced by one not as grand, but finally Herod the Great built a stupendous sacred enclosure which was completed only after his death and a few years before the Romans destroyed it. There were also synagogues for prayer and study, and after the fall of the Temple they were made on a larger scale. The Jews gradually overcame their scruples about pictures, and at least from the 3rd century A.D. synagogues were decorated with living forms.

Rather little of this art has been preserved to us except for the beautiful mosaic floors that are found in many parts of the country, for example at Tiberias and at Beth Alpha in the Jezreel valley. The artistic motifs are much influenced by secular and pagan models.

The same is true of Christian art. The mosaics of et-Ṭabgha covered part of the church's floor. They are unique. The large mosaic in the left transept is a celebration of the life of nature, done with humor and playfulness. Many of the pictures represent the flora and fauna of the Nile valley together with animals and plants found around the Sea of Galilee.

The mosaic of the loaves and fishes is of particular interest. It was originally behind the altar, but has been set in front of it for the enjoyment of worshippers and visitors.

Above the highway there are ruins of a 4th century church. Below it is a cave, which is evidently the one mentioned by Egeria as the place where Jesus spoke the Beatitudes. This seems curious because the sermon in Matt. 5-7 is said to have been delivered on a mountain or in the hill country, while Luke 6:20-49 is a partly parallel discourse spoken on a level place; and both a hill and a plain are located here. Fourth century Christians, however, had a predilection for caves as places of revelation.

The newer Church of the Beatitudes, a little to the north, is on a pleasant hill overlooking the lake. Its octagonal form honors the eight Beatitudes. The gardens are an excellent place for meditation.

At eṭ-Ṭabgha, nearer the shore, is a Franciscan church built in 1933 which celebrates the Primacy of Peter. This structure preserves the walls of a 4th-century church which commemorated the appearance of the risen Christ to the disciples (John 21:1-19).

IV. The Feedings of the Multitudes

Where did the earliest Christians believe that Jesus multiplied the loaves and fishes? Possibly at eṭ-Ṭabgha, though no one can be certain. We have to guess at what the four evangelists thought about the topography, if indeed they considered it at all, since their interest was in the religious meaning of the stories. All four gospels tell of the feeding of the Five Thousand, but the primary accounts are in Mark and John; the others are simply dependent on Mark.

John seems to picture the event on the "other" side of the lake, which usually means the east side. Afterward the disciples get into a boat and start for Capernaum. It is just conceivable that it was on the north side east of the Jordan, for to go from there to Capernaum would be a crossing of the lake. It is not quite clear what Mark had in mind. His several journeys across the lake might be only an artificial framework to connect the various stories, as many scholars think; but at times the structure seems coherent. Jesus' ministry in Mark begins in Capernaum, and he appears to be in Galilee—not the pagan Decapolis region to the east—down to 4:35. Now Jesus and his disciples start across the Sea of Galilee, a squall comes up quickly, the disciples are terrified, and the Lord calms the storm (4:35-41). They now arrive in the country of the Gerasenes, which is clearly on the east side, and Jesus restores a violently deranged man to sanity. The only difficulty comes at 5:21, when Jesus sails to "the other side"—and this can be only to the west, contrary to the usual meaning of "the other side"—because our Lord is obviously in Jewish territory when he heals the daughter of Jairus and the woman with the haemorrhage (5:22-43). He seems to stay in Galilee proper until the feeding of the Five Thousand (6:30-44).

If Mark knows the geography of Galilee and is conscious of it, he must place the feeding of the Five Thousand on the west side of the lake. He also tells a similar miracle, this time for the Four Thousand (8:1-10). In the meantime Jesus has been in the region of Tyre and Sidon, has returned through the territory of the Decapolis, a league of ten cities, which is east of the lake, and has healed a deaf mute. It is often suggested that Mark arranges his narrative symbolically, so that in the first instance the miracle of feeding is for the benefit of Jewish people, while the second is in a Gentile region.

V. Miracle

These are beautiful stories, wonderfully told. But what do they mean? More precisely, how do they touch the lives of pilgrims who visit the Church of the Loaves and Fishes?

Many Christians have no difficulty accepting the miracles of the gospels rather literally. Even so, this wonderful provision of food is not duplicated in our own experience. One can think of it as a sign of God's power and his Kingdom as manifested in that time and place, but that would be all. When people are hungry today, we share a little of our wealth and promote programs to meet immediate famine in Africa and for a better use of the agricultural resources of that continent.

Certainly this story implies sharing the five loaves and two fishes. But to "rationalize" the miracle, and say that everyone present followed Jesus' example and gave part of whatever he had, is to reduce it to a banal though edifying sermon. There is much more to it than that, and one ought to look into the rich symbolism of the story.

Mark says that the men sat down in groups like garden plots on the green grass, by hundreds and fifties. The figures suggest the organization of Old Testament armies, and one theory is that these were Galileans who wanted to go on the warpath and were looking for a leader—"sheep without a shepherd," as the Bible says of an army whose king has been slain. Perhaps Jesus would be their general! Mark, however, says that Jesus "began to teach them many things" and fed them only after that. Is it possible that he turned their minds away from revolution toward the Reign of God?

When Jesus was tempted to turn stones into bread, the gospel says that he answered the devil, "Human beings do not live by bread alone, but by every word of God" (Matt. 4:4; Luke 4:4). Not by bread alone, but men and women cannot exist without bread, or it may be rice. The story points to our two basic needs, spiritual strength and bodily sustenance. Jesus was accused of eating with tax-collectors and other outcasts. At such meals someone had bread, another person vegetables, perhaps olives and cheese, peasant fare. At the Last Supper, Jesus handed bread and wine to his companions.

The miraculous feeding is told much in the form of a celebration of the Lord's Supper or Eucharist. At the end the disciples, like deacons, gather up the food that is left. Mark no doubt believed that the bread and fish were multiplied miraculously, but he told the story for another reason: Jesus teaches and feeds all who are in need, and there is no limit to his bounty. When today we celebrate the Eucharist, we are taught in Scripture readings and in the sermon, we bring bread and wine and also money that will be used not just to maintain the Church but also to meet human needs in the worldwide community, and in turn we are fed and sent out into the world.

The mosaics at eṭ-Ṭabgha portray the bread and fish—universal symbols of Jesus—and the many animals and plants in the world which God created and which he loves and sustains.

6

The Message in Galilee

I

What did Jesus preach as he went through towns and villages on the east and west sides of the Sea of Galilee?

Because the gospel tradition was originally transmitted orally in the form of many brief stories and detached sayings, there is no way for historians to trace the development of his teaching. But perhaps it is reasonable to assume that when he began to preach and teach in Capernaum his message was already well formulated in his mind.

He spoke about the Reign of God; that is, God's loving and chastening activity toward his world and his People. The centre of his speech was always the living God in relation to humanity. This was set forth, not in logical propositions, but primarily in parables and other sayings that were like parables in that they were metaphorical.

God's Reign, the way in which he orders his world and relates to human beings, could not be described in ordinary language but only through stories that point to some aspect of that reality. The parables say in effect, "this is how it really is, even though most people do not think so."

These stories are drawn from everyday life in the Holy Land. They tell of some incident that actually occurred, or they may be typical examples of what often happens.

One might begin by considering the Sermon on the Mount (Matt. Chaps. 5-7). We know that this is a collection of sayings that Jesus probably uttered on various occasions, because Luke 6:20-49 is another collection resembling it, usually called the Sermon on the Plain. It would be natural if sometimes Jesus taught his disciples on a lofty hill, and the Mount of the Beatitudes is as good a place as any to imagine the scene.

Various Jewish prayers address God as "blessed" (*bārûkh*) —"Blessed are you, O Lord God, king of the universe." To be happy (*'ashrê*) is almost the same thing. Who has a blessedness that can be compared to the happiness of God?

The Beatitudes, which might be called "congratulations," are amazingly paradoxical. Matthew's tradition says that Jesus addressed the "poor in spirit" and "those who hunger and thirst for righteousness," while Luke reads "Blessed are you poor," "Blessed are you who are hungry now." The poor in spirit must be those who know their spiritual need. To thirst for righteousness means that one desires to be in right relationship with God and to lead the right life. But Jesus is also concerned for the physically poor and hungry.

These people also mourn, they are meek or gentle, they show mercy to others, are "pure in heart" (their minds are set on one important purpose); they are peacemakers, and they are persecuted. Such men and women will have the Kingdom of God and this includes all the rest of the promises: they will be comforted, inherit the earth, be fed and shown mercy, they will see God and be called his children.

In one sense these are promises for the future. God's Reign has not yet come completely to fulfilment—it is as though God is working toward this—but some of the benefits of his Reign are experienced even now as Jesus speaks and acts.

This is a message directed in the first instance to people in the Holy Land who are in misery, living either directly or indirectly under the often harsh rule of the Roman empire. But it comes also to men and women in more comfortable circumstances, who are under burdens of sin, sickness and anxiety. The Pharisees, who were the best element in the Jewish community, also had compassion on the common people, but little interest in sinners until they should repent and obey the Pharisaic interpretation of the law.

The Beatitudes could be heard as subversive. To speak of God's Reign might be to call for political independence— "no king but God!" Does this help to explain why Jesus was warned that Herod Antipas planned to kill him (Luke 13:31-33)? And although in the Sermon on the Mount, Jesus' sayings demand a change of heart, right motives leading to right action, he also had a way of interpreting the Old Testament law that was more simple, direct and radical than that of the Pharisees. For example, he seemed to be lax in interpreting the Sabbath law, and he rejected the complicated rules for purity. All this could lead to serious opposition.

II

We need to go to the parables to find out what Jesus meant when he spoke of God's Reign.

One group of parables emphasizes hope, the conviction that a new day has already dawned and that the future will be gloriously bright. The parable of the Sower (Mark 4:1-9) puts all the emphasis on the seed that falls on good ground and will bring a hundredfold crop. It is not clear that Jesus or God is the sower. Perhaps the seed is what happens here and now. Sometimes we see no result: seed falls among thorns or on a beaten path or a rocky ledge, but look at results of God's activity when soil is good!

There is another parable, this time about the patient farmer (Mark 4:26-29). We need not ask who the farmer is, he might be anyone. Once seed is sown, we go to bed at night and get up in the morning, but the seed is alive. God is in charge and doing what no human being can do.

These two stories have an element of surprise and wonder, even though they are examples of what can occur in real life. This is so with some other parables. The mustard seed is proverbially small, but it can turn into a great bush, almost a tree (Mark 4:30-32=Matt. 13:31-32=Luke 13:18-19). Yeast is even more mysterious. The ancients could not see this microscopic plant, nor did they understand its chemical action. It can make the dough overflow the pan (Matt. 13:33=Luke

13:20-21). In Jewish tradition leaven is usually a symbol for evil influence, and occasionally Jesus and Paul use it so (Mark 8:15; 1 Cor. 5:6-8), but in this parable the leaven is paradoxically a sign of God's Reign.

Jesus implies, though he does not say it in so many words, that God is involved in these natural phenomena. He puts the emphasis on the grandeur of the Kingdom of God and the hope that God guarantees.

III

Another group of parables evokes surprise in a different way. These suggest that in the world as God orders it, things do not turn out as most people conventionally expect them to do. The idea matches the words spoken in Isa. 55:8-9:

> My thoughts are not your thoughts,
>   neither are your ways my ways, says the Lord.
> For as the heavens are higher than the earth,
>   so are my ways higher than your ways
>   and my thoughts than your thoughts (RSV).

Paul expresses the theme by saying that the foolishness of God is wiser than human beings (1 Cor. 1:25) and "How unsearchable are his judgments and how inscrutable his ways!" (Rom. 11:33, RSV).

These parables which overturn expectations portray the world of human relationships rather than growth in the realm of nature.

There is the story of the workers in the vineyard (Matt. 20:1-15). The landowner is a crusty fellow and all business. Early in the morning he hires day laborers for the grape harvest at the going wage, and continues to enlist others during the day. The shock comes when in the evening those who have worked only one hour get the full wage but the men first hired receive no more. Now there is labor trouble, and the boss insists that he has a right to do as he wishes on his own property, and no one should complain if he is generous.

This is not a lesson in labor relations. There are theological explanations that many find attractive. For example, God's reward is not a matter of exact recompense, as the men who worked all day might think, but grace and generosity. Or, no matter how late the hour, one can always repent and come to God. One might say God can arrange affairs as he chooses; no one can question him. But the vineyard owner is not intended to be a perfect symbol of God; it is the whole parable, not the actors in it, that refers to God's Reign. There does seem to be a lesson that in this life we cannot expect reward according to our usual ideas of what is appropriate.

Yet the parable says none of these things explicitly. Instead it challenges and teases the hearers to think.

Chapter 15 of Luke contains three parables. The first two suggest how God goes out after sinners and rejoices when he brings them back (15:1-10). This evokes memory of Old Testament passages, for example "The Lord is my shepherd" (Ps. 23); God searches for his flock (Ezek. 34). The story of the woman with the lost coin brings the point closer if possible to everyday life.

The Pharisees of Jesus' time believed profoundly in repentance and forgiveness. But they did not actively seek out sinners and associate with them, as Jesus did and as the gospels indicate in several places (Luke 15:1; 7:34; Mark 2:15). Jesus' activity, and these parables, caused eyebrows to be raised.

The parable of the Lost Son (Luke 15:11-32) sharpens the issue. Again the father of the boys is just a father, not God. He was foolish enough to let his goods be divided and to give the younger son his share. The elder brother should not have acquiesced in this division; it is as though he wanted his own inheritance before his father's death. Yet there are always those who sympathize with him. His father had taken his loyalty for granted and had never given a party for him.

Then when the younger son comes back, ready to be only a hired servant, the old gentleman forgets all his dignity, runs to meet the boy, prepares a banquet and bestows on him new clothing and the ring which symbolizes lordship.

In only one way does the father suggest the character of God. That is the lavishness of his love and generosity. It has been well remarked that in Jesus' teaching there is a plus, a superabundance. One saying speaks of "a good measure, pressed down, shaken together and running over" (Luke 6:38). God brings rain and sunshine to the wicked and the good. Human beings, if they are to be true children of their father, must love their enemies (Matt. 5:43-48).

Christians who read the parable of the Pharisee and the Tax Collector (Luke 18:9-14) are apt to have little sympathy with the Pharisee. If they identify themselves with anyone it is with the repentant publican. But Jews think it unfair to categorize the whole party of the Pharisees in this way, because in the rabbinic tradition there are all kinds of Pharisees, and the best are those who act and live for the love of God.

The situation is more complicated than it seems at first sight, for there is a fine line between two possible attitudes. One can be deeply thankful for having been preserved from temptation; "there but for the grace of God go I." Or one can be complacent and compare oneself with the despised sinner. The Pharisee of the parable has evidently crossed this narrow and dangerous line. The issue Jesus has raised is not between Christianity and Judaism, or between Pharisees and penitent Jews. It cuts across the adherents of all religions, and too often the "Pharisee" ought to be understood as the "good church member."

Here, as in the other parables, Jesus is not so much interested in specific actions, good and bad, as in one's fundamental attitude toward life and its spiritual and moral issues. He also puts true humility, that is, honest and realistic assessment of oneself, high in his scale of values.

IV

Dominic Crossan has classified several of these little stories as Parables of Growth and Parables of Reversal. He understands a third group as Parables of Action, in which someone acts decisively.

The story of the Good Samaritan could be one of these (Luke 10:25-37), but it has other important aspects.

Another is so puzzling that when Luke wrote his gospel he was evidently not sure what its lesson was. This is the parable of the Dishonest Manager (Luke 16:1-8), and the little group of sayings that the evangelist placed at the end of it (16:9-13) offer a variety of interpretations.

When the manager is about to lose his job because of inefficiency or dishonesty, he resorts to a clever stratagem. He takes the IOUs that people have written when they bought wheat or olive oil from the estate and substitutes lower amounts. The debtors will now take him into their homes until he can find another position.

The story says that "the lord" praised this rascal. Is "the lord" the boss who was about to fire him? In this case the manager was not only shrewd but he also enabled his employer to get a reputation for generosity. But if "the Lord" is Jesus, the parable says in effect that the "children of light" should be as alert to their true business (the Reign of God or righteousness or the mission of Jesus) as this scoundrel.

In any case, the man acts.

There is also the parable of the Talents (Matt. 25:14-30) or the Pounds (Luke 19:12-25). Two of the slaves who have been entrusted with the money make a profit and are rewarded, but the third plays it safe, buries the funds, and returns them intact.

Why should this man be punished? The story must have disturbed some unimaginative people, because the apocryphal Gospel according to the Hebrews records a different form of it. The first slave earned money and was rewarded, the second hid the talent and was only rebuked, while the third squandered it with harlots and girls who played the flute, and he was put in prison.

Our English word "talent" is borrowed from this parable, and everyone understands one point in it. A talent, for mathematics or music or repairing machinery or whatever, is lost if it is not practiced and developed. But how did Jesus intend the story to be applied? We can only guess. Matthew appends a saying, "To everyone who has will be given and he will have abundance, but as to the one who does not have, whatever he has will be taken from him" (25:29). Mark 4:24-25 applies this to understanding the parables, and Luke 8:16-18 to revelation. Can it be that, if Jesus had his disciples in mind, they must make full use of the most precious thing entrusted to them, the message of the Reign of God? There are several accounts of how he sent them out to proclaim it. The most vivid, and perhaps the earliest of these, is in Luke 10:1-12.

V

The Reign of God, however, is not merely a message of hope to be preached. A follower of Jesus can "enter" or "inherit" the Kingdom of God. Such a one belongs to God, is under his lordship, or as the rabbis sometimes expressed it, takes the yoke of God's Kingdom upon himself or herself. That person is also a child of God, for God as King and God as Father are two sides of one coin. Jewish prayers sometimes address him as "our Father, our King;" when Jesus prayed he seems to have preferred the simple *Abba* (Father).

One can also "find" the Kingdom of God. As we read the gospels, we reflect that Jesus' words and deeds were a discovery to the people of Galilee. "A great prophet has been raised up among us! God has visited his People!" (Luke 7:16).

Twin parables about finding have been preserved to us. A man discovered a treasure in a field, hid it again, and in great joy sold everything he had and bought that field (Matt. 13:44). The ethics of what he did are irrelevant here; Jesus is telling a story only to make the point that he *found* and *acted.*

The parable of the Pearl of Great Price (Matt. 13:45-46) is an even clearer instance. This man was a pearl merchant, and when he sold his whole stock to buy this exceedingly precious pearl he was out of business. Or was he? Could he sell it at a huge profit? Jesus was not interested in such questions, only in telling his hearers: "This is the way it is with the Reign of God."

These twin parables have the elements of surprise and joy that are present in the Seed parables. They are also stories of reversal or change, a new situation; and finally they are examples of decisive action.

This action is costly. It requires taking a risk, as the slaves had to do when they invested the talents. Jesus asked his disciples to give up wealth and even family if necessary. One good man whom Jesus "loved" could not accept this and went away sorrowfully, for "he had great possessions" (Mark 10:17-22). St. Francis of Assisi heard the words as addressed to himself, gave away his patrimony, and went his way with great joy.

VI

Mark seems to have understood the healing of a man with an unclean demon as part of Jesus' teaching (Mark 1:27). On another occasion when he was accused of casting out demons through Beelzebul, he said, "If I by the finger of God cast out demons, the Kingdom of God has caught up with you," it is here (Luke 11:20; Matt. 12:28). Jesus taught the Five Thousand before he fed them.

Healing, forgiving sinners, and eating with outcasts were teaching through action. The kind of instruction that draws human beings out and develops them does not have to come in the form of words. These deeds of Jesus were part of that movement of God toward needy humanity which Jesus called the Reign of God. In short, he acted out what he said God was doing.

The tradition in Mark, Luke and Matthew indicates that while Jesus sometimes spoke about himself, more often it was about his mission, and most of all about God. The Father was central in his thinking, as in his prayer. He spoke of God mostly by allusion and indirection; to speak of his

Reign was to suggest how he operates in the world. We do not know about his inner life unless it is partly revealed in the Lord's Prayer, the parables, the stories of his baptism and temptation, and in a few words like this:

> Just now I was seeing Satan fallen from heaven like lightning (Luke 10:18).
>
> I have come to cast fire on the earth, and how I wish it were already aflame;
>
> I have a baptism to undergo, and how I am under constraint until it is finished (Luke 12:49-50).

7

Capernaum and Chorazin

I. Capernaum

Our English Bibles call the village Capernaum; in the Greek gospels it is Kapharnaoum. This was a Hebrew or Aramaic name *k^{e}phar Nahum*, village of Nahum, but we do not know to what Nahum could have referred. The Arabs named it Tell Hum, for it was only a tell, a mound, until the Franciscans excavated it. Their first discovery was magnificent, a synagogue in Graeco-Roman style. The doors face Jerusalem, and there are rows of pillars parallel to the walls. It is built of limestone, not basalt, and on the stones there is a wealth of decorative carving. The date may be as late as the 4th century A.D., though perhaps earlier, and it is not the one built by the Roman centurion who came to Jesus.

We have seen that early in his ministry Jesus settled in Capernaum, and Mark gives the impression of his continual activity in its region. The evangelist speaks of his preaching and teaching but tells more about his acts of healing. After the calling of the first disciples, the first scene is in the synagogue. Here he expels an "unclean spirit" from one of the men present. The people say, "What is this? A new teaching with authority!" Healing and teaching might seem to be separate aspects of his work, but just as God is one, so all of Jesus, activity was part of God's outreach to his people, meeting whatever needs they had. The Reign of God is coming, and its signs are already manifest.

There are accounts of Jewish rabbis who exorcised demons, but this type of healing is especially prominent in the gospel story. Evidently Jesus cured many people who had neuroses, psychoses and what we call psychosomatic illnesses. In many cultures people have believed that they were under the control of demons. Possibly the disturbed conditions of social life in 1st century Palestine made these symptoms more frequent, but one cannot be certain. The testimony of the gospels is that Jesus freed many people from such dreadful sicknesses, and that in this he recognized the inbreaking of God's Reign.

II. St. Peter's House

The Franciscans, who own the Capernaum site, have continued their archaeological work for many years. Not far from the lake they excavated an area that gives an idea of what the ancient village was like. They uncovered the foundations of a number of small houses, all of which had walls of black basalt. One of the finds is of special interest. It consists of an octagonal church which replaced a house church that Egeria saw. Underneath it is a dwelling. Very likely the early Christians venerated it as the house of St. Peter. It may have had only one story and a flat roof.

Mark, recounting the healing of the paralytic (2:1-12) says that four men carried the sick man up, dug through the roof and lowered him on his mat into the house. One can see a dwelling of this type in the Muslim Quarter of the Old City of Jerusalem. Poles are laid over the tops of the walls, branches are then strewn over these and the whole covered with mud. This explains the "grass on the housetop which withers before it is grown up" in Ps. 129:6.

One can easily imagine how, after leaving the synagogue where he drove out the demon, Jesus came into the house and healed Peter's mother-in-law who was lying on a bed suffering from a fever (Mark 1:30-31). The bed may have been no more than a pallet. People slept on the floor and wrapped themselves in rugs or similar coverings. In Jesus'

Plowing & Sowing: Taken on the tell of Bethsemesh in 1947.

parable of the Friend at Midnight (Luke 11:5-8) the peasant
says that he cannot get up to give his visitor bread because
the children are in bed with him. They were probably stretched out side by side on the clay floor of the house.

Not long ago the Franciscan archaeologists discovered the
ruins of a small synagogue very near the great building that
was first found. This was of basalt, and it may date to the 1st
century A.D. Rather few of the synagogues thus far uncovered in Palestine are so early, none of the oldest ones are
elaborate, and this is easily explained. A synagogue is not
essentially a building but a congregation. The *minyan*, which
must consist of at least ten men, can meet anywhere, in the
room of a building or even outdoors. The impulse to construct important structures for non-sacrificial worship in
Palestine came only after the Jerusalem Temple had been
destroyed.

Synagogue worship at this early date must have been
something like what went on in an old-fashioned Sunday
school. There were prayers, but the essential element was the
reading of passages from the Law and the Prophets and
when possible a sermon commenting on them. This worship
did not require presence of priests or learned scribes.

The Synagogue of Capernaum

III. The Centurion's Servant

Matthew (8:5-13) and Luke (7:1-10) give us the story of the Roman centurion who came to Jesus and asked him to heal his slave. One supposes that this officer commanded a hundred men of Herod Antipas' troops. Such a prince had soldiers primarily for police purposes, but Josephus tells us that once Antipas was defeated in an engagement with Aretas IV, king of the Nabataeans. The war broke out because Antipas had divorced Aretas' daughter in order to marry Herodias, a marriage that John the Baptist had denounced (Mark 6:17-18).

The centurion, being a pagan, did not know how he would be received by a Jewish holy man. "I am not worthy," he said, "to have you come under my roof." Luke, in fact, says that he first asked the local elders to intercede for him, and these men explained, "he loves our nation and he himself built a synagogue for us." It is possible that Luke's tradition had in mind the small building found by the excavators.

The story is charming. The centurion said, "You have only to speak a word and my servant will be healed. I am a man set under authority, and I have soldiers under me;" that is, I know how to take orders and to give them. But the principal point is Jesus' final remark, "Not even in Israel have I found such faith."

Evidently Jesus had considerable success in this neighborhood, but he did not always encounter faith. He is quoted as saying bitterly,

> Woe to you, Chorazin, woe to you, Bethsaida, for if the mighty deeds done among you had been done in Tyre and Sidon, they would have repented long ago in sackcloth and ashes...
> And you, Capernaum, will you be exalted to the heavens? You will be cast down to Hades.
>
> (Luke 10:13-15=Matt. 11:21-24).

IV. Chorazin

The lament was over Chorazin and Bethsaida as well as over Capernaum. There is a rabbinic saying that even the idle curse of a holy man is effective. One dislikes to think of Jesus as uttering such a condemnation, and some scholars conjecture that these woes were spoken by a later Christian prophet in the name of Jesus. Yet it must be remembered that our Lord spoke out against evil—especially hypocrisy, cruelty to "little ones" in the name of religion, and complacency. There was nothing weak or sentimental in his nature. His moral strength went along with his compassion and sensitivity.

At any rate, all three towns disappeared. Throughout history wars, changes of population, the silting of rivers and ports, volcanoes and earthquakes have destroyed cities. After the Muslim invasion, Judaism and Christianity were no longer dominant in the Holy Land, and no one cared about these villages.

Chorazin lies on a hill two miles north of Capernaum. Eusebius, bishop of Caesarea in the 4th century, the first great historian of the Church, says that he found only ruins here. The city, including its synagogue, was rebuilt in the 5th century, evidently after an earthquake. Chorazin does not figure in Christian history, but it was an important middle-sized Jewish town which occupied as much as 80 to 100 acres. The Talmud says that it was famous for its wheat. Now it is waste land, but in ancient times the farmers made it productive.

Since 1980, excavations have been resumed. Israeli archaeologists have reconstructed the fine synagogue so far as possible, particularly the entrance, Torah niche, and the reader's platform with its "seat of Moses," on which there is an Aramaic inscription. The roof was originally supported by twelve columns, some of which are monolithic. Several have been re-erected with their architraves. It is not certain whether there were galleries over the side aisles.

The layout of the synagogue is similar to the one in Capernaum, with doors facing Jerusalem, and many intricate carvings in something like Byzantine style. Like all the other buildings in Chorazin, it was constructed from basalt, which is much more difficult to carve than limestone. It may have been built in the late 3rd or early 4th century, This was a period when Judaism flourished in Galilee.

Only a small part of Chorazin has been uncovered. Near the synagogue, which is in the centre of the city and on the main road, the archaeologists have excavated two complexes of dwellings, a public building, and a ritual bath. An olive oil press found in the north part of the town may be as early as the 2nd century A.D.

Few places along the lake evoke such a sense of desolation. There is no wheat here, only thorns and weeds. In its present state, one thinks of deserted places in the hill country where Jesus went to pray in solitude (Mark 1:25, 45; John 6:15; Luke 6:12). Yet Chorazin may have been occupied as early

as the Neolithic period (6000-4000 B.C.), for in the neighborhood there are many dolmens—huge basalt blocks, two
placed upright with a third serving as a roof. Such monu-
ments were evidently burial places.

8

Bethsaida and the East Side

I

Strictly speaking, the Jordan river was the eastern boundary of Galilee and the jurisdiction of Herod Antipas ended there. It was natural, however, that ancient people sometimes spoke of the eastern shore of the lake as part of the region. Thus the Gospel of John says that Andrew, Peter and Philip came from Bethsaida of Galilee (1:44; 12:21). "The other side" was largely pagan, but some Jews undoubtedly lived there.

Bethsaida was barely east of the Jordan. The place that usually bears the name was located about two miles north of the Sea of Galilee. Its tell stands 295 feet above the surface of the lake. It was already inhabited, and the tetrarch Herod Philip, son of Herod the Great and half-brother of Antipas, made it into a city and named it Bethsaida Julias in honor of Julia, the daughter of Augustus.

That emperor honored Herod's will by granting to Philip a large, sparsely settled territory north and east of the Sea of Galilee. Luke 3:1 calls this region Ituraea and Trachonitis. It extended as far north as Caesarea Philippi at the foot of Mount Hermon. Part of it is now known as the Golan Heights.

It was important to the Roman empire to have all this region ruled by princes who could be trusted, and the sons of Herod were loyal allies.

We do not know how much information about topography the evangelists had, or whether they aimed to be precise. As we have seen, Mark locates the feeding of the Five Thousand somewhere near Capernaum and then says that Jesus sent his disciples to "the other side" to Bethsaida (6:45). But Luke 9:10 locates this miracle somewhere near Bethsaida.

The sequel in Mark is the eerie account of how the disciples were on the lake, rowing desperately in the face of a storm wind, and late at night Jesus came to them walking on the water (6:45-51). The Lord greeted them with the words, "Take courage, I am," which recalls the "I am" in Yahweh's revelation to Moses (Exod. 3:14-15). Bracketed with the miraculous feeding, this story was a sign to the church for which Mark wrote his gospel that, no matter how late the hour, how great the peril, Jesus is with his Church.

The Bethsaida of the gospels may not be Bethsaida Julias at all, but a fishing village on the north shore itself. This is a place which now has the Arabic name el-'Araj, and it has a natural port. In 1972, accompanied by my archaeologist friends, Alix and John Wilkinson, I tried to walk to the place, but marshes and lagoons made it impossible. Probably the only way to reach it is by boat.

II

Mark tells of an unusual journey of Jesus to the regions of Tyre and Sidon (7:24). These are famous historical cities. Sidon (Saida) lies about 25 miles north of Tyre in Phoenicia. It was sometimes independent, but it was destroyed by the Assyrians, later by the Neo-Babylonians, and very terribly by the Persians in 351. It surrendered to Alexander the Great and had a measure of independence under his successors, the Seleucids of Syria. In Pompey's time it came under Roman rule. Sidon was famous for its glass and for the purple dye produced there. The Romans broke its monopoly of the latter product. Jesus is said to have preached to people from this city (Mark 3:8).

Tyre (Ṣur) was on a small island near the borders of the tribe of Asher. Like Sidon it manufactured glass and purple. Its king Hiram, who traded with Solomon (1 Kings 5; 9:26-28), built a breakwater there, and Tyre had one of the best harbors in Phoenicia. Alexander conquered it only after a bitter seven-month siege and took 30,000 people as slaves. He built a mole which has permanently connected it to the mainland.

Somewhere in this region Jesus healed the daughter of the Syrophoenician woman (Mark 7:25-30). This is very important for Mark's understanding of Jesus' ministry, for it taught that the Good News had come to Gentiles also. Our Lord returned to the Sea of Galilee through the Decapolis (7:31).

The Decapolis ("ten cities") is a league of city states. These were organized on the Greek model; Greek was spoken there, and the culture was at least superficially Hellenistic. The cities were founded after the conquests of Alexander the Great and were important as bases of power for the Seleucid monarchy of Syria and later for the Romans. Damascus, Philadelphia (now Amman in Jordan), and Scythopolis (Bethshean, Beisan) in the Jezreel valley, all important cities, belonged to this league. Gadara, Gerasa and Hippos, to be mentioned later, are others. The boundaries of these city-states are not certain. Philip's authority presumably did not extend to them but only to the villages and country districts outside them, but his influence would have been great.

The first incident Mark mentions after Jesus' return through the Decapolis is the healing of a deaf-mute (7:31-37), which leads the people to exclaim, "He has done everything splendidly; he makes the deaf hear and the dumb speak." The symbolism of this is obvious; it is a sign of the power of the Good News, and recalls a prophecy in the Book of Isaiah:

> Then the eyes of the blind shall be opened,
>   and the ears of the deaf unstopped;
> then shall the lame man leap like a hart,
>   and the tongue of the dumb sing for joy
>
> (Isa. 35:5-6, RSV).

The story of the deaf-mute is followed by the feeding of the Four Thousand (Mark 8:1-10), after which Jesus and the disciples cross the lake to Dalmanutha, a place otherwise unknown (Matt. 15:39 has "Magadan"). But at this point "the Pharisees" demand a "sign," perhaps to test Jesus' authenticity, and he and his disciples return to the east side (8:13). Now there is a discussion with the disciples over leaven, loaves of bread, and the miracle that they have just witnessed. Readers may be puzzled by this passage, but the essential point of it has to do with the blindness of the disciples. Jesus says, "You have eyes but do not see, and ears but do not hear" (8:18).

Now the stage is set for Jesus and his company to come to Bethsaida. The healing of the blind man (8:22-26) is told in much the same way as the story of the deaf-mute. It is important to note that the man receives his sight in two stages: first imperfectly, because he sees human beings "as if they were trees walking," and then with complete clarity.

The full meaning of this will emerge when we consider the account of Peter's confession at Caesarea Philippi.

III

North and east of Bethsaida's marshy shore the land is firm enough to be cultivated. This dry land continues along the east of the lake. It is a narrow strip below the hills where the Golan Heights begin. A little to the south are some remarkable ruins uncovered a few years ago by Israeli archaeologists.

These were a monastery and a church built by Greek-speaking monks about the middle of the 5th century A.D., almost certainly to commemorate Jesus' exorcism of an insane man (Mark 5:1-20). The complex is surrounded by a plastered wall which at one time was decorated by pictures. The gate faces the lake, and from it a pavement runs to a quite large church with a main aisle and two side aisles. Mosaics covered the sanctuary floor. One of the rooms to the southeast was later made into a baptistery, and a mosaic inscription dates this to 585. There is also a burial crypt below the church.

The monks' living quarters were to the north. Also north of the monastery there are ruins of a small village at the lakeside which had a port with a breakwater. This is one more indication of how thickly settled the region was in ancient times.

Mark's story of the miracle is vivid and dramatic. The man was violent and uncontrollable and possessed by a "legion" of demons; one immediately thinks of Roman armies. Expelled by Jesus, the demons ask to enter a herd of pigs, and these now plunge down a cliff and are drowned in the lake. A little south of the church there is a cliff that fits the story.

The miracle and its setting are important to Mark. At the end of the story we find the man clothed and in his right mind, asking to follow Jesus. But whereas our Lord usually orders that his healings be kept secret, on this occasion he bids the man to go to his own people and tell them how many things the Lord (the true God) has done for him. This man was a pagan; it was Gentile territory, for pigs were kept here. Thus the story prefigures the mission to the Gentiles.

The Arabic name of this place is el-Kursi. The word can be understood as "the seat" or "chair," but this does not suggest anything definite. Mark says that the miracle took place "in the region of the Gerasenes." Gerasa (Jerash) was a great city, many miles to the east, and we do not know that its territory reached so far west. Some important manuscripts of Mark substitute "Gergesenes," and this seems to be the correct reading in Luke 8:26. It is not clear how "Kursi" could be derived from this; Kursi could be a corruption of Korazim (Chorazin), and St. Jerome confused the latter with this site on the lake.

Matthew, in a parallel story, calls this the country of the Gadarenes (8:28), and "Gadarene swine" has become a proverbial phrase. Gadara is certainly nearer than Gerasa to el-Kursi, but it is still several miles away to the southeast at a place now named Umm Qeis.

Gadara has some interest because it is a prime example of how deeply Hellenistic culture had penetrated this region. The city lay on a hill five miles southeast of the Sea of Galilee. Its territory included the hot springs known as Hammath Gader which were famous as a health spa in the 1st century and have been visited for healing ever since. Gadara had all the amenities of a Greek city such as a colonnaded street and two theatres. It was the birthplace of several important literary men, one of whom was the erotic poet Meleager, many of whose verses are to be found in the *Greek Anthology*.

IV

About five miles south of el-Kursi is Ein Gev, where tourists enjoy the pleasures of the Sea of Galilee. Above it are ruins of another city, Hippos or Susitha (both names seem to mean "city of horses"). Pompey gave it the rank of a city of the Decapolis and had it rebuilt with streets in the usual Roman grid pattern. Later Augustus granted Susitha to Herod, but after his death it reverted to the province of Syria. It was on the Roman road from Scythopolis to Damascus. One might suppose that if el-Kursi belonged to any city-state it could have been Hippos.

9

Caesarea Philippi

I

A visit to Caesarea Philippi brings pilgrims into northern Galilee and beyond. It will begin on the main road north from Tiberias. After a few miles one passes Rosh Pinna, an old Jewish settlement that takes its name from Ps. 118:22,

> The stone that the builders rejected has become the head of the corner (*rosh pinna,* perhaps "keystone" or "cornerstone").

From this point a road goes off to the left to Safad or Zefat, a city famous in Jewish tradition as the home of mystics who studied the secret writings of the Kabbala. For this reason it was considered one of the holiest cities in the land. Now it is also an artists' colony, and it is often pointed out as "a city set on a hill that cannot be hid" (Matt. 5:14). Some other villages in Palestine would serve equally well.

North of here one can take either of two routes. Going directly north, one comes first to Hazor, on the left. This was an important Canaanite city which the Israelites conquered. It has been extensively excavated. On the right of the road are the Hazor museum and the kibbutz Ayeleth ha-Shahar, which has a guest house and a restaurant. The name of this place comes from the superscription of Ps. 22, which prescribes a tune for singing it, "Hind (Deer) of the Dawn." It is said that in the early days of the kibbutz someone shouted this phrase to awaken the residents.

A little farther north is an extremely fertile plain which was once a shallow lake through which the Jordan flowed. This was called Lake Huleh, and in Hellenistic times Semechonitis. The area is intensively cultivated, with fruit orchards and other crops, as well as pools for carp. Before the lake was drained, water lilies, papyrus and other reeds grew in it. The valley as a whole measures about 15 miles from north to south, and is from four to six miles wide. The principal town in the region is Qiryat Shemona.

Ancient Dan is beyond here, near the road to Caesarea Philippi. The Old Testament writers thought of this as the extreme northern part of the Holy Land, which stretched "from Dan to Beersheba." According to the Book of Judges, the tribe of Dan left the coastal plain and conquered the old city of Laish. After the kingdom of David and Solomon (about 1000-922 B.C.) broke up when Jeroboam I revolted against Rehoboam, Jeroboam set up "golden calves" in two sanctuaries, at Dan and Bethel. At Dan, excavation has uncovered walls, a monumental city gate, and a high place for worship.

The stream from the largest of the three sources of the Jordan flows past Dan.

It is possible that Jesus and his disciples followed the route just mentioned when they went to Caesarea Philippi.

An alternative way to go is by taking a road that branches off to the right north of Rosh Pinna. This crosses the Jordan at the bridge of the Daughters of Jacob, and the ancient Way of the Sea from Egypt to Damascus may have followed this route. Jewish people sometimes identify these "daughters" as those of the patriarch Jacob, but the name seems originally to have been given to Greek Orthodox nuns of a convent dedicated to St. James (= Jacob) that once existed nearby. The road goes through the northern part of the Golan Heights to Quneitra, a Syrian town occupied by the Israelis since the 1967 war.

This region is a high basalt plateau, in which small cones of extinct volcanoes are to be seen here and there. When

Augustus set up Syria as an imperial province controlled by himself, Herod the Great was not given a realm as large as the old Maccabaean kingdom. But he was awarded Gaulonitis (the Golan Heights), the territory around Lake Huleh, and the town later named Caesarea Philippi. After Herod's death part of the area passed to his son Philip.

Gaulonitis was never thickly settled, although the basaltic soil was fairly fertile. Some Jews who lived here fought in the war of A.D. 66-73. In the 2nd and 3rd centuries of our era there were many Jewish settlements.

Beyond Quneitra there are magnificent views of Mount Hermon. This mountain is the southern spur of the Anti-Lebanon range and its summit is about 9,100 feet above the level of the Mediterranean. Snow covers it through much of the year, and often it is shrouded in clouds. The Old Testament mentions it several times, sometimes naming it Sirion. Pagan texts call it a sacred mountain, and a Greek inscription has been found honoring the god of the mountain. It lies at what are now the borders of Lebanon, Syria and Israel.

The route goes through several Druze villages. These are a peculiar and warlike people with their own religion, which is an offshoot of Islam although they deny being Muslims. The Druzes call themselves by a name that means "Unitarians"; they try to keep their doctrines secret, but actually much is known about them.

The cult originated in the early 11th century when a teacher proclaimed that the caliph al-Hakim was an incarnation of the divine cosmic intelligence. Everything proceeds from the One, and knowledge of the One is the only way to salvation. The Druzes teach that there have been several incarnations, and venerate a number of prophets, with special reverence paid to Jethro, the father-in-law of Moses, who is supposed to be buried below the Horns of Hattin near Tiberias. Their privileged teachers wear white turbans and are known as the "wise."

Muslims have often persecuted the Druzes, and there is some hostility between adherents of the two religions. A number of Druze villages exist in Galilee, and many of the men have fought in the Israeli army. Other Druzes in Syria are enrolled among the Syrian troops. This is not strange, for sometimes these people have warred with one another as well as against outside enemies.

II

In ancient times many cities were named Caesarea in honor of some emperor, and sometimes the names persist today, as at Caesarea on the seacoast, already mentioned, and Kayseri in Turkey.

Caesarea Philippi lies 1,150 feet above sea level. Its Arabic name is Banyas, and this preserves a name that Greeks must have given it shortly after the conquests of Alexander the Great. From very ancient times it was evidently a spot where water and fertility gods were worshipped. The Greeks dedicated the cave, out of which flowed one of the sources of the Jordan, to Pan and the nymphs, as we know from an inscription found on the site. They named the cave the *Paneion* and the town Paneas.

Because of later earthquakes, the waters no longer emerge from the cave but from a crack below. The cave of Pan is decorated with carvings, and there are niches in the cliff beside it where statues were once placed.

This locality is of strategic importance. It was here, about 198 B.C., that the Seleucid monarch of Syria, Antiochus III the Great, defeated the Egyptian armies of Ptolemy V and gained control over Palestine. The Maccabees never conquered this district. When the emperor Augustus turned it over to Herod the Great, that Jewish king erected a temple here in white marble, and dedicated it to his benefactor. After Herod's death the tetrarch Philip ruled it until A.D. 34. This man enlarged and beautified the city and named it in honor of the emperor Tiberius and himself. Later the locality became part of the realm of Agrippa II, who was a son of King Herod Agrippa I (A.D. 41-44; Acts 12:1-23); Paul gave his defense before the former (Acts 25:13—26:32). After the first Jewish revolt, Titus celebrated his victory at Caesarea Philippi.

Roman bridge and city gate, Caesarea Philippi

The city continued to be important throughout the 1st century. Its population was always predominantly pagan.

III

It was a dramatic moment when Jesus and his disciples came here. As the great geographer Sir George Adam Smith remarked, here in this centre of paganism Peter acclaimed Jesus as the Messiah of the one true God.

Mark makes this episode the centrepiece of his gospel. It comes in abruptly after the healing of the blind man of Bethsaida. This restoration of sight in two stages must surely set the scene for Peter's confession of faith and the epiphany of the Transfiguration. Jesus' nature is now gradually revealed to the disciples. Their blindness is cured; even so, they still do not understand the full meaning of what they see. From this point on, everything in Mark's gospel moves toward the Crucifixion.

What the evangelist has done is to bring several traditions together in the passage 8:27—9:1 and to tell the story in such a way as to make it a living challenge to the people who first heard or read his book. Jesus first asks, "Who do people say that I am?" The disciples answer that some identify him as John the Baptist and others as Elijah or one of the prophets. Jesus pursues the question further—"What do you say?"— and Peter responds, "You are the Messiah." At this Jesus immediately orders the disciples not to speak about him, or perhaps to say nothing about his messiahship. Then he goes on to say, somewhat enigmatically, that the Son of Man must suffer, be rejected, die, and rise again.

There was no single concept of "Messiah" in Judaism. The idea of Messiah ("anointed one") as an ideal king descended from David is the earliest known to us, but in the Maccabaean period (about 163-63 B.C.) the Testaments of the Twelve Patriarchs, documents preserved to us in Greek, give evidence of belief in a Messiah from the tribe of Levi, to which the Maccabaean family belonged. The Dead Sea Scrolls contain various ideas: a priestly Messiah and the (lay) Messiah of Israel (1QSa); a prophet like Moses (Deut. 18:18-19) who is also the star out of Jacob (Num. 24:15-17) (4Q175); but also the Davidic Messiah (4Q174). Melchizedek is a deliverer also, but is not called Messiah (11QMelch).

In considering the passage in Mark we must think of two situations, as though we had a photographic double exposure here: the moment at Caesarea Philippi, and Mark writing a gospel for the Church. As the dialogue may have been spoken originally, the word "Messiah" implied a king descended from David who had the power of God behind him and who might drive the Romans out—by military force if necessary— and restore independence to the Jewish nation. To say that Jesus was Messiah was, therefore, dangerous. It was all that Jesus' enemies needed to use against him, and already there were many men ready to enlist under the banner of a royal pretender. But, far more than this, such a role was not Jesus' destiny. He would not and could not be that kind of Messiah.

The second situation is this: when Mark wrote, "Jesus is the Messiah" was the universal faith of Christians. But what did these words mean? It was well known that he had been crucified and was risen. Yet the Cross was still a problem. Was it only a temporary setback in Jesus' march toward glory or only a part of the inscrutable will of God? Indeed there were Christians, later to be considered heretics, who believed that Jesus did not really suffer. The Resurrection had meaning for Christians, but what about the Cross?

Mark was evidently saying something like what Paul had already taught in different language, that the way of the Cross was not for Jesus alone but also for everyone who professed to follow him. There might be victory and glory ahead, but it was only for those who could take up the Cross. If Peter or anyone else should reject this demand it meant to be on the side of Satan.

IV

Now comes the story of the Transfiguration. The theme of blindness and restoration of sight continues. The man of Bethsaida had been healed in two stages. Just so here, after the partial unfolding of the mystery at Caesarea Philippi, Peter, James and John are permitted to see Jesus more clearly. But even after this, Mark continues to portray the disciples as imperfect followers—just as the Church's leaders of his own time were too often blind—and it is only after the Resurrection that Peter and the others will be able to discern the nature of Jesus in its full dimensions.

The event is told in most striking fashion so as to call to mind several passages in the Old Testament. The six days, the high mountain, the shining of Jesus' face, and the cloud are all in the story of Moses on Mount Sinai (Exod. 19:16; 24:15-18; 34:29-35). Elijah and Moses, according to Jewish tradition, did not die but went directly to heaven. The "tabernacles" or tents suggest the Festival of Booths. In Jesus' time this was as important as Passover and was connected with hopes for the glorious restoration of Israel. But the voice from heaven proclaims not the law but Jesus himself, and the words are similar to those spoken at his baptism. In all these ways the account expresses the authority of Jesus as Son of God and the glory that he will have when he returns as Son of Man.

One can only speculate on what lies behind this story, which is expressed in terms of the theology of the early Christians. Peter and men like him had minds that were ready to see visions and hear prophetic voices. The three disciples may have had an overwhelming experience on the mountain.

The context in Mark's gospel suggests that the evangelist was thinking of Mount Hermon, the highest point in the Holy Land. No other place could rival Sinai for the sense of the mysterious and the sublime.

V

Eusebius thought of both Mount Hermon and Mount Tabor as possible locations for the Transfiguration, but St. Cyril of Jerusalem, whose influence must have been immense, declared for Tabor. It was certainly more accessible than Hermon, which few pilgrims could ever have climbed. The beautiful dome-like shape of this mount attracted people with pious sentiments, and Tabor could be seen from many places in the land.

This mountain lies six miles east-southeast of Nazareth and about twelve miles from the Sea of Galilee. The plain below it adjoins the Jezreel valley. The Book of Judges tells how the Canaanite chariots were mired in the mud near the foot of Tabor and the Israelites under Deborah and Barak won a victory (Judg. 4:12-16; Chap. 5). Many battles were fought on and around the mountain. From the summit there are magnificent views in all directions—the mountains of Upper Galilee, Mount Hermon, the Horns of Hattin, the plain of Jezreel, the Carmel range, and the mountains of Samaria.

Nain and Mount Tabor

From time to time Muslim armies have driven Christians from the place, but for some centuries now the summit has been occupied by Greek Orthodox and Latin Catholics, who have churches and convents there.

Another reason why Tabor was chosen as the site of the Transfiguration is that, according to Mark, when Jesus came down from the mountain he found his disciples in discussion with "scribes" (9:14). Would Jewish teachers have been present in the pagan region of Mount Hermon? It is here that Jesus healed the epileptic boy (9:15-29), and many preachers have remarked that our Lord's first act was one of mercy. It was also an occasion to teach his disciples. Tradition locates this miracle at the village of Dabburiya. After this Jesus went through Galilee (9:30) and arrived in Capernaum (9:33).

VI

Not far from Tabor is the Arab village of Nein, which preserves the ancient name Nain. It is attractive as seen from the road, perched as it is on the slope of a hill between Tabor and Mount Gilboa. Endor, where King Saul consulted the medium (1 Sam. 28:3-19), is only two miles away. There are only 200 inhabitants in Nein now, but ruins nearby show that it was once a larger town.

This is the location of one of Luke's most touching stories (7:11-17). A dead man is brought out to the gate of the city, the only son of his widowed mother; and Jesus raises the young man to life. "And he gave him to his mother," just as in the stories of Elijah (1 Kings 17:23) and Elisha (2 Kings 4:36). Shunem, where the latter miracle occurred, is in the same region. Little wonder that the people of Nain exclaimed, "A great prophet has risen among us! God has visited his people!"

10

Samaria

At some point Jesus left Galilee for the last time. As Mark tells it, after the healing of the epileptic boy he was in Galilee only incognito (9:30). The evangelist now records some of his teachings, and then Jesus goes east of the Jordan (Mark 10:1). After this Chapter 10 consists of incidents enshrining his teaching, except that at one point, as they were on their way to Jerusalem his disciples are stricken with awe and fear, and Jesus predicts his Passion for the third time (10:32-34). At last the group suddenly appears at Jericho (10:46).

The account in Matthew is similar (Matt. 19:1; 20:29) except that more of Jesus' teaching is included. Luke, however, records only three short episodes (Luke 9:44-50) before Jesus "sets his face" to go to Jerusalem (Luke 9:51). In this gospel Jesus goes into Samaria or at least to its borders (9:52), and he is still in Galilee when he learns of Antipas' threat to kill him (13:31). Later on Luke remarks that on his way to the Holy City he passed between (or through the midst of) Samaria and Galilee (17:11), and finally he heals the blind beggar as he is approaching Jericho (18:35-43). Luke seems to visualize a journey through the northern part of Samaritan territory down to the road on the west bank of the Jordan and entrance into Jericho from the north.

Thus Luke says nothing of a route through Transjordan, while Mark and Matthew know nothing of a ministry in Samaria.

A careful reading of Luke 9:51—18:35 shows that there is no particular structure in this section. It is a very important collection of Jesus' teachings, containing parables and other items not found elsewhere. By writing his gospel in this fashion, Luke has artistically indicated a long journey and a lapse of time, but the geography is vague.

This section, however, exhibits a definite interest in the Samaritans. On the one hand, Jesus is rejected by a Samaritan village because he is evidently on the way to Jerusalem (9:51-56). On the other hand, a Samaritan is the hero of one of his greatest parables (10:30-37).

II

The Gospel of John gives an entirely different picture. Jesus' public ministry begins in Galilee, but soon he comes to Jerusalem for Passover (2:13). He is in Galilee again when he heals the royal official's son (4:43-54), but in Chapter 5 the scene is Jerusalem and in 6:1—7:9 it is Galilee, without anything said about Jesus' travels. Finally he goes to Jerusalem for the feast of Tabernacles (7:10). With few exceptions, then, John thinks of Jesus' important activity as taking place in Jerusalem and other parts of Judaea, with two or three journeys north to Galilee.

One of these trips is through the Samaritan region, when Jesus has his significant encounter with the Samaritan woman at Jacob's well. Samaria is important to Luke and John.

Modern Israelis often speak of their country as comprising Judah, Samaria and Galilee, plus the coastal area and the Negeb to the south. The three main areas are distinct geographically and historically. "Samaria" in this sense corresponds in the main to the territory traditionally allotted to the Joseph tribes, Ephraim and Manasseh. This is the central highland region, with high hills and deep fertile valleys.

King Saul (about 1010 B.C.) came from the tribe of Benjamin. His palace was just north of Jerusalem, and his realm extended through this country to the north, although he fought some battles in the south. When David first established his kingdom he ruled at Hebron as king of Judah, but afterward was accepted as king of Israel by the elders of the north. Thus he ruled two kingdoms and it was a personal union. Jerusalem, which he conquered, was his own possession, not a part of either realm.

David and Solomon tried to unify the kingdom and extended their conquests over a wide area, but the stupid tyranny of Rehoboam led to a disruption in which Jeroboam the son of Nebat became king of Israel (about 930 B.C.). It is noteworthy that a prophet encouraged Jeroboam to revolt. Later on the kings of Judah were able to add Benjamin to their territory, and in the days of the divided monarchy there were two tribes in the southern kingdom and theoretically ten in the north.

David and his successors encouraged a theology which celebrated Mount Zion (Jerusalem) as the place of God's presence. The northern tribes held to an older concept, that their nation was a league of semi-independent tribes. The prophets of the north remembered the covenant on Mount Sinai rather than the special covenant with David. The northern kingdom had shrines at Dan and Bethel and later on Mount Gerizim, near Shechem. The Judahite writers of the Scriptures regarded all such places as contrary to the will of God.

The kingdom of Israel was relatively rich and had a series of kings, some of whom were quite successful. But no one dynasty endured, while all the kings of Judah belonged to the line of David. The independent spirit of the north made it possible to replace one monarch with another, and sometimes prophets assisted in a coup d'état. Thus Elijah received an oracle ordering him to anoint Jehu (1 Kings 19:15-16), and his successor Elisha saw to having this done (2 Kings 9).

Several of the prophets denounced these Israelite kings for their compromise with the fertility worship of the Baals, and also for their alliances with foreign powers. But it was Assyria that finally brought the northern monarchy to an end, deported many of the people to Mesopotamia and Persia and settled Assyrians in Israel (722/721 B.C.; 2 Kings 17:1-6,

24-34). This region now had a mixed population. Yet worship of Yahweh continued in some fashion.

Judah in turn fell to Nebuchadnezzar in 587 B.C. and many of its inhabitants were deported. After about 70 years exiles began to return. Ezra (458-457) and Nehemiah (445-432 B.C.) tried to keep Judah separate from Samaria and ordered Jews (Judahites) who had married Samaritan women to divorce their wives.

From this time on, relations between Samaritans and Jews were strained and gradually deteriorated. The Samaritans must have continued some connections with the Jews long enough for them to have the Torah, the so-called five books of Moses (Genesis through Deuteronomy) as their Scripture, in fact their only Bible. But the final breach between the two nations may have come only after the conquests of Alexander the Great when a temple was erected on Gerizim. Excavations have shown that such a sanctuary was built in the Hellenistic period. This was destroyed by the Maccabaean king John Hyrcanus in 128 B.C. A later temple was constructed in the time of the emperor Hadrian (2nd century A.D.).

III

Theologians and other religious people are selective in what they hate. The sharpest hostility is often between two groups that are almost alike, so that one side considers the other heretical or schismatic. A totally different religion does not constitute so great a threat, but when there is a strong feeling for dogmatic purity, deviants are feared and disliked. So Yeshua ben Sira, author of the book called Ecclesiasticus or Sirach, wrote:

> With two nations is my soul vexed,
> and the third is no nation:
> Those who live on Mount Seir [the Edomites],
> and the Philistines,
> and the foolish people that dwell in Shechem
> (Ecclus. 50:25-26).

The Mishnah reads, "He who eats the bread of the Samaritans is like one who eats pork." Some legal rules of the rabbis treat Samaritans as though they were Jews, others as though they were Gentiles.

The Samaritans must have been an embarrassment. There were prophecies in Scripture that God would bring back all his people, including the "lost" ten tribes, and were the Samaritans not part of these?

The fascinating story of the Samaritan woman (John 4:1-42) illustrates this situation. When Jesus asks her for a drink of water, she is surprised. "How can he, since he is a Jew, ask for water from a Samaritan, and especially from a woman?"

The scene is at Jacob's well, just below and to the east of ancient Shechem. John says that the woman's village is Sychar. There is a village a little east of the well, known by the Arabic name Askar, and Eusebius seems to have identified such a place; or Sychar may have been another name for Shechem.

Certainly the well now shown to visitors is the one mentioned in the gospel. It is, as the woman said, very deep, about 115 feet. A church built here in the late 4th century was destroyed in 529; later the Crusaders erected a new church. In 1914 the Greek Orthodox began to reconstruct this, but the work has never been finished. According to Gen. 33:19-20, Jacob bought a plot of ground at Shechem and erected an altar; later he was buried here. This may explain why the well was attributed to Jacob.

The story of this meeting with the Samaritan woman is interesting in several respects. Throughout John's gospel Jesus is presented as somewhat aloof and in command of every situation, but here he is tired out and thirsty. At the same time, Jesus uses this condition of his to teach. The woman's learning is only gradual. Jesus speaks of living water which satisfies thirst permanently, but "living water" can mean running water, and the woman understands it so. How good it would be if she no longer had to draw from this ancient well! Jesus then, in the dialogue about her husbands, shows his supernatural knowledge.

As a result she recognizes the visitor as a prophet, and her curiosity is piqued. Perhaps he can settle the ancient controversy between Jews and Samaritans as to where the true temple should be located; but Jesus now takes the opportunity to speak of a new universal worship in spirit and in reality.

Like the Jews, the Samaritans believed in a messianic figure whom they called the Ta'eb; and the woman says, "Oh, well, when he comes he will explain everything to us." Jesus then announces that he himself is the Messiah. She drops the water pot and summons the people of her village.

IV

Here we are introduced directly to the early Church's mission to the Samaritans. John has told the story with this in mind, as one can see from Jesus' remarks to his disciples: "Lift up your eyes and look at the fields, for they are white for the harvest ... One sows and another reaps."

From the evangelist's point of view, Jesus had sown the seed. The Samaritan people now come and hear the Messiah, and as they come to faith they say to the woman, "Now we believe, not just because of what you have said; we ourselves have heard him, and we know that he is truly the Saviour of the world."

According to the Book of Acts, the effective mission to the Samaritan region began when Philip, one of the Seven (Acts 6:5) went to Samaria and proclaimed the message of Christ with great success (8:5-13). One of these baptized was a magician named Simon, and after a visit from the Jerusalem apostles resulted in signs that the new converts had received the Holy Spirit, Simon tried to buy the gift of imparting the Spirit. Peter, of course, denounced him (8:14-24).

This is only one tradition about this mysterious Simon Magus. Acts had explained that he had claimed to be "someone great" and that many people in Samaria said of him, "This is the power of God called Great" (8:9-10). Other traditions, preserved by the Church Fathers Justin Martyr and Irenaeus, make him out to be a dangerous heretic who had ideas associated with Gnosticism and who travelled about with a woman named Helena. It is impossible to know just what Simon did and taught, but he was probably an historical person and somehow involved in the gnostic movement which orthodox Christians rejected.

V

Shechem is a very old city. There was a village here in the Chalcolithic period (ca. 5000-3150 B.C.). An important city state was founded here in the Middle Bronze Age (ca. 2200-1550 B.C.), and this was refounded after a destruction in the Late Bronze Age (ca. 1550-1200). There have been extensive excavations, and the ruins include two city gates, massive walls and two temples, a private one for the ruler and another for the people. The city is connected not only with Jacob's story but also with that of Abraham, who camped here and was promised the Holy Land (Gen. 12:6-7). It was also the place where Joshua summoned all the tribes and had them promise allegiance to faith in Yahweh (Josh. 24). After the disruption of the kingdom, Jeroboam I made Shechem his capital. Later the royal seat was moved to Tirza and then to Samaria. The city was never settled again after John Hyrcanus destroyed it.

After this destruction the people who had inhabited Shechem must have lived in villages on and near the ancient site. Five or six miles to the northwest of it was the site of Samaria, which had been the capital in ancient times. Herod the Great built a temple here in honor of the emperor Augustus, the splendid ruins of which can be seen today, and named the place Sebaste (*Sebastos* is the Greek equivalent of the Latin *Augustus*). Although this was a pagan foundation, some adherents of the Samaritan religion probably lived in its neighborhood.

Certainly the Samaritans were very numerous and under the Roman empire they generally flourished. In A.D. 36 a crowd of them assembled when one of their number promised to find the sacred vessels that Moses was supposed to have hidden on Mount Gerizim. Pilate stupidly had these people massacred. The Samaritans complained to the emperor, and Pilate was removed from office.

Then in A.D. 72, after the first Jewish revolt, the Romans founded a colony just west of ancient Shechem for the veterans of Titus' army and named it Flavia Neapolis. The present large town of Nablus, peopled by Arabs, is on this site and preserves the Roman name. The great Christian apologist of the 2nd century, Justin Martyr, was the son of one of these settlers. By this time Christianity had taken root in the region.

For some centuries the Samaritan religion continued to prosper. The emperor Hadrian permitted the temple on Gerizim to be rebuilt. But the Samaritans were under pressure from Jews, and also from Christians, particularly after Christianity became the official religion of the empire. The Arab invasions brought further trouble; the Samaritans lost converts to Islam and were sometimes persecuted.

In modern times the sect dwindled, and two generations ago there may have been only 180 living Samaritans. More recently the number has increased, and there have been some intermarriages with Jews. The community benefits from visits of tourists and pilgrims, and the State of Israel has been benevolent toward it. Most of the people live in Nablus and a smaller number in another town.

Since the 19th century the Samaritans have been able to celebrate the Passover according to their ancient customs on Mount Gerizim. Tourists are permitted to see only the slaughter of the lambs, not the actual feast.

VI

The Gospel of John says at one point that John the Baptist was baptizing at Aenon near Salim (3:23). "Aenon" simply means "springs," and there is a place called Salim about five miles east of Shechem.

If we suppose, with Luke, that Jesus came through Samaritan territory on his way to Jericho, he may well have followed the principal road from Nablus toward the Jordan valley, which was a Roman road in the 1st century. On this route one can see on the left a convenient place for baptisms, even though it is not Aenon. A copious spring gushes out near the road, and the water sparkles in the sunshine. A few years ago a local resident was using it to cool Coca Cola and other soft drinks which he offered for sale.

11

Jericho

I

On his last journey to Jerusalem, Mark indicates that Jesus went to the east side of the Jordan; he would have crossed somewhere south of the Sea of Galilee and made another crossing at one of the fords of the river. But Luke gives the impression that he approached Jericho from the west side of the river. In the latter case the road followed a wady down to where the present Adam or Damieh bridge is located. It was here that Joshua and the Israelites first entered the Promised Land. Near this spot they ate the Passover and set up the sanctuary at Gilgal (Joshua 3-4; Ps. 114:3-6).

If we were to follow this route, we could see on the right the Alexandrium, one of the fortresses built by Herod the Great. Farther on, and nearer Jericho, is the traditional place where John baptized the multitudes in the river, and Jesus himself received baptism (Mark 1:1-11).

II

What was the purpose of John the Baptist when he announced a "baptism of repentance for the remission of sins"? Judaism employed ritual washings to remove various kinds of impurity. The Essenes, who had their community centre southwest of Jericho, were particularly given to this practice, both when men entered the sect for the first time and on other occasions.

We know, too, that when proselytes (converts) became members of the Jewish religion and nation, they were first instructed in the commandments, the men were circumcised, and baptism completed the process of becoming a Jew. It is sometimes thought that John was saying, in effect, that the Jews of his time were little better than pagans, and needed a thorough repentance and purification.

Or he could have been inspired by Psalm 51 or by the words of Ezekiel, in which God said:

> I will sprinkle clean water upon you, and you shall be clean from all your uncleannesses, and from all your idols I will cleanse you. A new heart I will give you, and a new spirit I will put within you ... and cause you to walk in my statutes and be careful to observe my ordinances (Ezek. 36:25-27, RSV).

This prophecy refers to the last days, when all Israelites were to be brought home from their places of exile. John taught that the time was very short before God would come to judgment.

For our knowledge of John, we are almost completely dependent on the New Testament and other Christian sources. These show that the Baptist gathered a group of disciples, not all of whom became Christians (Luke 7:18; John 1:35; Acts 19:1-7). Josephus tells us also that in the Jordan valley there were other teachers who baptized; he himself had spent some time with one of them named Bannus.

But John was not like the Essenes. Although like them he had disciples, the Essenes were a closed community who kept themselves apart from other Jews. John made his appeal to the nation as a whole.

Did Jesus need to repent? This question seems to have perplexed early Christians, for they considered him sinless (Heb. 4:15). Thus Matthew 3:13-15 records a dialogue, in which John exclaims, "I need to be baptized by you, and are *you* coming to *me*?" Jesus answers, "Let it be so; it is proper for us to fulfil all righteousness" (i.e., to do every right act).

There is also a curious passage which St. Jerome quotes from the lost Gospel according to the Hebrews,

> The mother of the Lord and his brothers said to him, "John the Baptist is baptizing for the remission of sins; let us also be baptized by him." But he said to them, "In what have I sinned, that I should go and be baptized by him? Unless perhaps this very thing that I have said is an ignorance."

Ancient people, and especially Jews, found their identity and the meaning of their lives as members of a group. Jesus was no isolated individual; his life was bound up with that of his fellows. As a loyal member of God's people he took part in what was intended to be the corporate repentance of Israel.

John may have chosen the place of baptism because of its symbolic significance. It is near the crossing into the Promised Land, and Gilgal was a place of covenant and new beginnings. Everything here suggests renewal of the holy community.

But much more happened when Jesus was baptized. Mark says that he saw the skies torn apart and the Spirit descending like a dove, and a voice came from heaven, "You are my Son, the beloved, in you I take delight" (or "I have chosen you") (Mark 1:10-11).

III

As one approaches Jericho from the north, one comes first to the great spring known as 'Ain es-Sultan, which has always supplied the town with water. To the right is Tell es-Sultan, the mound of the most ancient Jericho. Dame Kathleen Kenyon excavated this place and found that it was first settled in the Neolithic age before the invention of pottery, about 8300-6000 B.C., and this means that Jericho is the oldest *continuously* inhabited city so far known on earth. The reason is obvious: the climate, the source of water, the fertility of the soil made it a good place to live.

Joshua had to capture Jericho in order to gain possession of the Promised Land. Miss Kenyon was not able to find the wall that fell down on this occasion; it may have been made of mud brick which would disintegrate.

From the top of the tell one can see a high hill to the west, the traditional Mount of Temptation. The local Arabic name for this is Jebel Quruntul, Mountain of the Forty, because the gospels say that Jesus fasted and was tempted for forty days.

The story in Matt. 4:1-11 and Luke 4:1-13 says that the devil made three suggestions to him. First, to turn stones into bread. He would not only satisfy his own hunger, he could feed anyone who was starving. Second, he might throw himself down from the pinnacle of the Temple and thereby prove to everyone, himself included, that he was truly God's Son. Third, he was taken to a high mountain to see all the kingdoms of the world and their glory. If only he would follow Satan, he could be a world monarch. Jesus answered all these impulses with an apt word of Scripture.

No mountain, and certainly not this small one west of Jericho, is high enough to see all the kingdoms. By saying that the tempter showed them to Jesus "in a moment of time," Luke indicated that this could only be in imagination and in the Spirit. The subtle words of the tempter symbolize the actual temptations that Jesus had to undergo during his ministry.

Other religions tell stories of how their founders and saints were tempted at the beginning of their ministry. The pattern makes sense psychologically: an overwhelming experience of vocation, the need to be quiet and to fast and prepare oneself, the inevitable perplexities and temptations.

Between the 4th and 6th centuries of our era, when Christianity was respectable, popular, and no longer persecuted, men who were not satisfied with the increasingly worldly Church fled to the Jordan desert to live in monasteries or as hermits. At one time there were 130 settlements of monks in this region. But it was only in the 12th century that the mountain near Jericho was claimed to be the place of Christ's temptation and churches were built, one in a cave and the

Excavation of New Testament Jericho

other on the summit, in a place that had been a fortress in the Maccabaean period. From this height there are magnificent views of the Jordan valley, the Dead Sea, the mountains of Moab, the rocky desert of Judaea and the tower on the Mount of Olives.

IV

More than any other place in the Holy Land, Jericho illustrates its many periods of history. We do not know what language the earliest inhabitants of Tell es-Sultan spoke or who they were. They may have had an idea of life after death, for they molded clay over the skulls of dead people to make them appear more lifelike. The tell was abandoned after the exile to Babylon. Thereafter Jericho may have been little more than a village, until fortresses were built in the Maccabaean period. Herod the Great built a palace and a hippodrome-theatre near the place where the Wady Qelt comes down to the valley, and new aqueducts to irrigate the area.

The large modern town, populated by Arabs, is on a site apparently first settled in the Byzantine period. Jericho flourished at this time, and two Jewish synagogues have been uncovered in the region. The Muslim Arab armies conquered Palestine in the 7th century A.D. and in the following century the land was ruled by caliphs of the Ummayad dynasty. One of these, probably al-Walid ibn Yazid (743-744) built a hunting lodge a little north of Jericho, walled in a great park, and began a palace. Lavish decorations were discovered when the ruin, Khirbet el-Mefjer, was excavated in 1947-48. In the 12th century, when the Crusaders ruled the Holy Land, sugar cane was cultivated at Jericho.

When the Franks were defeated and withdrew from Palestine, irrigation canals were abandoned and the city declined. Only after World War I did Jericho begin to revive as a fruit-growing region. The oranges are of high quality.

Luke gives the impression that Jesus entered Jericho from the north. He tells of the healing of a blind beggar as he approached the city (Luke 18:35-43); then as Jesus came through Jericho he saw the tax collector Zacchaeus, who had climbed a tree. Jesus, far from rejecting this man, asked to stay at his house, and this led to the man's repentance. Zacchaeus promised to restore his ill-gotten gains fourfold (twice what the law required) and to give half his goods to the poor (19:1-10).

Visitors are shown a tree which the local residents say Zacchaeus climbed. This is only a pretty fancy; at that time Jericho seems to have been located west of here.

V

Whatever settlements there may have been in the Jericho region in the time of Jesus, it is certain that the main part of the city was near a winter palace that Herod constructed. He had another such place at the fortress of Masada, on the west side of the Dead Sea and near its southern end.

Mark Antony, who ruled the Roman world for a few years, gave Jericho and its region to Cleopatra. The two were defeated at the battle of Actium in 31 B.C. and afterward they committed suicide. Herod the Great first leased Jericho from Cleopatra, and when Octavian (Augustus) became master of the empire he granted this territory to Herod.

One of the Maccabaean kings, perhaps Alexander Jannaeus (103-76 B.C.), had built a palace at the point where the Wady Qelt ended. Here an aqueduct brought water to fill a large swimming pool. Herod constructed buildings on both sides of the wady. One of the most remarkable structures on the south consisted of two porches with columns linked by a facade in the Roman brick work known as *opus reticulatum*. On the north there were a palace, swimming pool, ritual baths and other structures.

He also had a large theatre and hippodrome built at Tell es-Samrat, southwest of the mound of Tell es-Sultan.

Herod died at his Jericho palace of a painful and loathsome disease, and he was buried in a tomb he had planned at the Herodion, southeast of Bethlehem.

I have previously mentioned Luke's story of the healing of the blind beggar. He probably rewrote the vivid earlier account in Mark 10:46-52 which names the man as Bartimaeus. If so, Luke located this at Jesus' entrance into Jericho for artistic reasons. But, according to Mark, this incident took place as Jesus was leaving Jericho. This would be near Herod's palace, and just as the disciples and their Master were about to begin the hot, weary ascent toward Jerusalem. We are told that Bartimaeus followed Jesus on the road. He had become a disciple.

VI

The Jericho of Herod and Jesus stands at a kind of geographical boundary where much of the surrounding region is visible. The contrasts are sharp—the fertile oasis of Jericho, the jungle-like Jordan valley, the rocky wilderness of Judaea where only drought-resisting plants can survive, and the Dead Sea, the lowest point on the earth's surface. Life and death are close together. To the south are the concrete houses of a huge Arab refugee camp whose inhabitants fled to Jordan and other Arab countries after the 1967 war.

The region west of the Dead Sea was, as I remarked, a place where many monasteries were founded in the Byzantine era. One of these, Mar Saba, has been occupied continuously since it was founded in A.D. 482, and a few Greek monks live and worship there. It is on the banks of the Kidron wady which begins southeast of the Temple area in Jerusalem. Pope Paul VI restored the bones of the founder, St. Sabas (439-532) to this place, and St. John of Damascus (died 749), one of the greatest theologians of the Orthodox Church, is buried there also.

Long before this time, indeed in the days of Jesus and before, there was a community centre of the Essenes near the northwest shore of the Dead Sea at a place known by the Arabic name of Khirbet Qumran. These were the people who wrote the Dead Sea Scrolls. A beduin shepherd boy named Muhammad edh-Dhib discovered the first of these in what came to be known as Cave 1, and in 1947 brought them to an antiquities dealer in Bethlehem. Later Père de Vaux of the Dominican École Biblique and the Jordan Department of Antiquities excavated Qumran. Meanwhile the Beduin of the Ta'amireh tribe searched the whole area, and they and the archaeologists found other manuscripts and many fragments.

Because this was the most important discovery in modern times of written materials in Hebrew and Aramaic, and the documents came from the period just before and after the ministry of Jesus, the Scrolls have provoked an immense amount of discussion. We are certain that the people who wrote them were the Essenes whom Josephus mentioned and who interested even the Roman writer Pliny the Elder. Some questions were asked immediately. What can be the relation of these people to the other Jews of the time? Do the discoveries throw any light on the teaching and ministry of John the Baptist and Jesus and the writings of the New Testament?

The Essenes were a sect. In contrast, the Pharisees and Sadducees were parties within Judaism. Despite their differences, they had to be in interaction and to work together to some degree, whereas the Essenes withdrew from association with other Jews as much as possible, and they rejected the sacrifices in the Jerusalem Temple as impure.

Josephus says that some of them lived in the cities of Palestine, and it appears from their books that at one time a group of them settled in Damascus. Their principal centre was, however, at Qumran. The members lived in nearby caves, cultivated a small oasis nearby, and came to the centre for communal meetings, worship and study. The complex of buildings includes cisterns, baths for ritual purification, a kitchen and refectory, a pottery workshop, and—most significantly—a writing room where the archaeologists found a large plastered table and two inkwells.

The Essene movement may have begun in Babylonia, where many descendants of the exiles lived for centuries. If so, some of its members returned to the Holy Land in order to practice their religion fully. In any case, a group settled at Qumran about 150 B.C. under the leadership of a person whom they called the Teacher of Righteousness. This man, who may have been the author of the Manual of Discipline or Community Rule, one of the most important of the scrolls, was in opposition to the "Wicked Priest." Very possibly it was this bitter struggle which led the group to Qumran, where some centuries earlier there had been a fortress.

Scholars disagree as to who the Wicked Priest might have been. One suggestion is King Alexander Jannaeus, who was known for his warlike exploits and opposition to the Pharisees. But Jonathan and Simon, brothers of Judas Maccabaeus, who acted as high priests, are other possibilities. They belonged to a priestly family but not to the Zadokite line, and for this reason the Essenes would have rejected any of the three.

The Essenes are remarkable first of all for their ability to adapt to desert conditions. They built a dam in the Wady Qumran and arranged it so that water could flow through a tunnel into an aqueduct and from it into a series of cisterns. Rain falls only a few times each year in this region, but this ingenious system allowed enough water to be collected to last for many months. Below Qumran there is also a small green oasis with a spring now called 'Ain Feshkha which permitted a little intense cultivation.

The community resembled later Christian monasteries in some respects. A period of probation was required before membership, goods were held in common, and there was a hierarchy, with the priests in a superior rank. Most Essenes did not marry; the few who took wives did so only to pro-create children. The motive for celibacy was the desire to be in a perpetual state of purity in accordance with biblical regulations. This was an unusual sort of piety, for elsewhere in Judaism the priest had to keep these rules only at certain times, and all men were normally expected to marry.

Thus the Essenes were a sect and a religious order. They also had a military character, for one of their strangest books, the War Scroll, gives ritual and tactical directions for a holy war. The Essenes had rules for personal hygiene derived from Old Testament laws applying to an army on a campaign (Deut. 23:12-13).

Although these people expressed hostility to other Jews, the enemy in the War Scroll is the Kittim, a word that means "Greeks" in the Old Testament, but now was applied to the Romans. The war that the Essenes expected was a final triumph over these evil forces. This would be the climax of history.

One reads the Essene literature with a certain sense of pathos. It reveals great earnestness and unrealistic hopes that were not to be fulfilled. Like many zealots in history, these men were fervidly religious. Some of their meals, per-haps all of them, were sacred. The time not spent in main-taining their livelihood was passed in prayer and study of the Scriptures. They copied biblical books and other Jewish re-ligious literature that never became part of the Bible, and they composed commentaries on many books of the Old

Testament, interpreting them as prophecies of their own community and its history. The Temple Scroll, one of the last to be published, is a program for the Temple and the Holy City that they hoped would be a reality in the end-time. In a way it is a revision of parts of Ezekiel and other books.

The Hymns of Thanksgiving and parts of the Manual of Discipline disclose the piety of the Essenes. Their concern was always for obedience to the sacred law, but this was also a religion of the heart. The Essene was conscious of his mortality and weakness, and God's giving of the law was an act of grace, love and redemption. There is a warm aspiration toward God. At the same time, the Scrolls have an almost paranoid character. The authors, who are the children of light, are menaced by the children of darkness. In the end their only hope is to obey the law and to be prepared to fight in the confidence that God is on their side and will bring victory.

The history of the sect, so far as it can be reconstructed with certainty, begins in the turbulent days of the Maccabees. Their buildings were badly damaged by an earthquake in 31 B.C. and the site was abandoned for about thirty years; where they went in the meantime we do not know. But they were at Qumran for most of Jesus' life and remained there until the Romans expelled them in A.D. 68. Evidently some of the Essenes were among the Jews who made their last stand at Masada and died there in A.D. 73 or 74, for fragments of their books were found in the excavation of that fortress.

Evidently the movement died out, though its influence may have persisted for a time in some Jewish circles.

In many ways these people were like the Pharisees but more strict. Their literature shows some interesting parallels with passages in the New Testament, but we are not certain whether the language and ideas are Essene or simply Jewish. Jesus does not seem to have been influenced by them. In contrast to their separateness, he proclaimed his gospel openly, lived his life within the larger Jewish community, and had little concern for the purity regulations. His method of quoting the Hebrew Bible was not like that of the Essenes, and his message had a different spirit and tone.

12

The Road to Jerusalem
and the Triumphal Entry

I

There is now a good road from Jericho to Jerusalem. Much of it was improved after 1948 with the aid of United States funds, when the West Bank was ruled by the Kingdom of Jordan. It is possible to turn off and travel part of the older road, although tourist buses avoid it. Here one can see across the deep Wady Qelt the spectacular monastery of St. George of Koziba.

This began early in the 5th century as a small oratory where hermits living in nearby caves came to celebrate the Eucharist. Toward the end of the century a monastery was built. When the Persians invaded the land in 614 they destroyed much of it as well as many Christian shrines in Jerusalem, and it was not rebuilt until the time of the Byzantine emperor Manuel Comnenus I (1179). There were other reconstructions between 1878 and 1901.

One of the legends that grew up in the 12th century is that the prophet Elijah stopped here on his way to Mount Horeb. The biblical account in 1 Kings 19 says only that he went from Jezreel to Beersheba and thence to Horeb. Pious people in the middle ages may have confused this story with one earlier in the book, according to which Elijah was fed by ravens at the brook Cherith, a wady east of the Jordan (1

Kings 17:1-7). At any rate, this visit by Elijah is commemorated by a cave church adjoining the monastery which is dedicated to the saint.

The road from Jericho to Jerusalem has the biblical name of the Ascent of Adummim. It is surely an ascent, for it begins about 850 feet below sea level and climbs to an elevation of about 2,500 feet above. This road was on the northern boundary of Judah (Josh. 15:7; 18:17).

The original meaning of *Adummim* is not quite certain. Some scholars interpret the name as "scorpion pass," but the popular translation is "ascent of blood" because of the red soil to be seen near the Khan (caravansary or inn) of the Good Samaritan. This ruin is not the inn mentioned in the parable (Luke 10:30-37), and it may have been a fortress built by the Knights Templars. In fact, Jesus may have had no specific place in mind. The story was probably his creation for the purpose of making a point, but the attack on the traveller was typical of something that occurred all too often. Certainly in the 19th and early 20th centuries, people were often plundered and killed by bandits. We visited Jericho on December 27, 1947 and returned safely to Jerusalem, but two hours later a car was ambushed by bandits on this road.

II

John Wilkinson, former director of the British School of Archaeology in Jerusalem, has studied the old Jerusalem-Jericho road. The route taken by Jesus and his disciples probably followed the line of a highway that the Romans later paved. This was north of the new road which leads to Jerusalem through Bethany.

Mark 11:1, which is our oldest source, reads: "When they drew near to Jerusalem, to Bethphage and Bethany, at the Mount of Olives, he sent two of his disciples .... " The chapel now known as Bethphage, where Palm Sunday processions begin, is between Bethany and the village on the summit of the hill known as eṭ-Ṭur. On this basis one would expect Mark to say "to Bethany and Bethphage," not the reverse. But eṭ-Ṭur, where the Russian tower stands, is probably the original Bethphage, and Mark probably thought of Jesus as going directly over the Mount of Olives, not turning aside to Bethany.

Mark now tells of the preparations for Jesus' triumphal entry into Jerusalem (11:2-7) in such detail that it gives the impression that some eyewitness told what had happened, but did not explain it. Jesus ordered two of his disciples to go into the village opposite (perhaps Bethphage) and bring a colt to him. "The master (the Lord?) has need of it," and the bystanders made no objection. The evangelist may have assumed that Jesus had supernatural knowledge, but it has also been suggested that he already had friends in the village who would lend him the colt without question.

This is the first subtle hint that this is a royal entry, for monarchs often impressed horses into service.

Now begins the entry itself. The disciples place their garments on the beast to make a saddle for Jesus. Others spread their garments on the road together with branches—perhaps from nearby trees or other plants—and shout a verse from Ps. 118.

The gospel writers think of this event as occurring a few days before Passover, yet the story suggests ceremonies celebrated at the time of the Tabernacles festival in the autumn. This comes in the month of Tishri after the other high holy days, New Year and the Day of Atonement. It was always a harvest festival and one of the three great annual pilgrimages. The command to live in booths of myrtle and willow for a week commemorated especially the wandering of the Hebrews in the wilderness (Lev. 23:39-43; Deut. 16:13-17).

The celebration had several fascinating features; for example the Hallel psalms (113-118) were sung, and at certain points the worshippers waved the *lulab,* branches of myrtle and willow with a sprig of palm, and the *ethrog* or citron, which they carried.

Psalm 118 seems originally to have been a king's song of thanksgiving after he has been victorious in a dangerous battle. Christians, as early as New Testament times, applied it to Christ, and it has deeply influenced Christian worship.

Verses 25-26 read:

> Save us now (*hoshi 'a na*), we beseech thee, O Lord!
>   O Lord, we beseech thee, give us
>   success!
> Blessed is he who comes in the name
>   of the Lord!
> We bless you from the house of the Lord.

There is no evidence, other than the gospels, that these ceremonies were observed at Passover time, though they were a feature of the Feast of Rededication in December, which was modelled on Tabernacles. As the gospel story goes, a crowd suddenly formed here on the Mount of Olives, and sang the psalm verses with significant alterations:

> Hosanna! Blessed is he who comes in the name of the Lord!
> Blessed is the coming kingdom of our father David!
> Hosanna in the heights! (Mark 11:9-10).

What does "Hosanna" mean in this context? Is it a prayer to God, "Save us now, O thou who art in the heavens?" When everything is considered, it seems that the people were doing more than performing a familiar ritual. They welcomed Jesus as the Messiah son of David, soon to be king, and prayed that God would save the nation.

In one parallel, John 12:13, Jesus is acclaimed as king of Israel. Matthew makes explicit an idea that is implied in Mark's story: Jesus is fulfilling a prophecy of Zechariah,

> Tell Daughter Sion,
> See, your king is coming to you,
> gentle and coming on an ass,
> on a colt, the foal of an ass (Matt. 21:5; Zech. 9:9).

Here we observe the paradox that runs through all the gospel story. Jesus is the true king of Israel, but he disdains the use of force; he does not come on horseback but like a peasant teacher on a donkey. What we do not know is why he chose to *ride* into the Holy City instead of walking. Did he encourage or at least permit this demonstration?

If word of the event came to the attention of the authorities, they might well have considered Jesus a dangerous person.

Mark says only that he entered the Temple area, looked around at everything, and since it was evening, went out to Bethany with the Twelve.

Professor Benjamin Mazar of the Hebrew University in Jerusalem, who excavated the areas south and west of the Temple enclosure, told me that he believes Jesus would have entered the area from the south, through the triple Huldah gate, which is now blocked up, but whose portals are visible.

III

Jerusalem was the goal of many pilgrimages. From early times it has had a powerful emotional appeal. The Psalms glory in it.

> Great is the Lord, and highly to be praised; in the city of our God is his holy hill.
> Beautiful and lofty, the joy of all the earth, is the hill of Zion, the very center of the world and the city of the great King. . . .
> Make the circuit of Zion; walk about her; count the number of her towers.
> Consider well her bulwarks, examine her strongholds, that you may tell those who come after
>
> (Ps. 48:1-2, 12-14, *Book of Common Prayer).*

Most religious Jews consider Jerusalem and the return to Zion to be part of their theology; for unbelieving Jews, Zionism is a political ideology. The whole land is sacred and Jews tend to regard it as their eternal possession. Muslims, because of their traditions, make a similar claim. Muhammad ascended to heaven from the Rock after a miraculous flight from Mecca. The el-Aqsa mosque is the third holiest spot on earth. From one point of view, any place can be holy where the Father is worshipped "in spirit and in truth" (John 4:23-24), but for Jews and Christians, as for Muslims, there are sites in the Holy Land and elsewhere with associations that recall saving events and evoke faith and thanksgiving. Jerusalem is a holy city for Christians also. The attitudes of pilgrims can have great variety. When Kaiser Wilhelm II visited Jerusalem, part of the wall around the Jaffa Gate was removed so that he could ride in on horseback. Lord Allenby conquered the city on what has been called the Last Crusade, but he decided to enter on foot.

Ezekiel cried out, "Woe to the bloody city!" (24:6). In the period before the exile it had been precisely that, it has known war in most of the centuries since, and at the present time we see no real prospect of peace. Yet we continue to say,

> I was glad when they said to me,
>   "Let us go to the house of the Lord."
> Now our feet are standing
>   within your gates, O Jerusalem ...
> Pray for the peace of Jerusalem;
>   "May they prosper who love you.
> Peace be within your walls
>   and quietness within your towers ..."
>   (Ps. 122:1-2, 6-7, *Book of Common Prayer*).

and exiles have sung many times:

> If I forget you, O Jerusalem,
>   let my right hand forget its skill.
> Let my tongue cleave to the roof of my mouth if I do not
>   remember you,
>   if I do not set Jerusalem above my highest joy
>   (Ps. 137:5-6, *Book of Common Prayer*).

Jerusalem lies on the central ridge of the country. Like the territory west of it, it is Mediterranean in climate, fauna and flora. The ridge is a rain maker but it is also a rain barrier.

Jerusalem—Old City; Kidron Valley on left.

As I remarked previously, one has to go only 3 or 4 kilometres east of the Mount of Olives to be in steppe country.

The city is off the main highways, and it has no natural economic importance. It is not as important strategically as Haifa and Megiddo. People care for Jerusalem for historical and religious reasons.

Pottery from the Chalcolithic period (4000-3200 B.C.) has been found here, and in most prehistoric times Jerusalem had some population. Egyptian texts of the 19th and 18th centuries B.C. mention it as Urushalim. The name may mean "foundation of Shalem," a long-forgotten god. The city first comes into our traditions in the curious chapter 14 of Genesis, which says that Abraham met Melchizedek, king of Shalem, priest of God Most High. He also prepared to sacrifice Isaac on Mount Moriah, which 2 Chron. 3:1 identifies with the Temple mount.

Joshua was not able to take Jerusalem, though he captured and mutilated its king Adonibezek. It was not allotted to the twelve tribes. David captured it because someone was able to climb through a water shaft or tunnel and get into the city (2 Sam 5:8; 1 Chron. 11:6 ascribes the feat to Joab). Jerusalem was ideally suited to David's purposes. His first city was south of the present Old City on the Ophel hill, which had been Jebusite Jerusalem. Later on Solomon built his Temple on a higher elevation, where the Dome of the Rock now stands.

13

Jesus in Jerusalem According to John

I. First Visit to Judaea

Matthew, Mark and Luke tell of only one visit of Jesus to Jerusalem except that Luke gives us the charming story of the twelve-year-old boy in the Temple. The situation in John, as I have remarked before, is entirely different. Immediately after the marriage in Cana, this evangelist tells of our Lord coming to the city at Passover time and "cleansing" the Temple.

The Church Father Origen, in the 3rd century, remarked that there is no way to reconcile the gospels so as to produce a chronological account of Jesus' ministry. All that we can do is to read the several stories and try to understand their inner meaning. In this Origen was wiser than many people who have attempted to write a "life of Jesus."

If one compares the story in John 2:13-22 with Mark 11:15-19 it becomes evident at once that the Fourth Evangelist has given a theological interpretation. This in fact was his method throughout his gospel. He has also located most of Jesus' ministry, especially his confrontation of opponents, in Jerusalem and Judaea. Yet he probably preserves a sound historical tradition that Jesus was in Jerusalem two or three times prior to his last fateful journey.

When we ask about Jesus' daring action against the money changers and the vendors of sacrificial animals, it seems more likely that this occurred on the last visit than on the first. At this point it is well to look at John's story line and its geography. For example, John has located Jesus' highly theological discussion with Nicodemus (3:1-10 or 3:1-21) on this first visit to the city.

Jesus seems next to be somewhere near John the Baptist, who is baptizing at Aenon near Salim (3:22-30). This is not actually in Judaea. Three places have been claimed to be this Aenon. One is a little west of the Jordan and eight miles south of Scythopolis (Beth-shean). A second is on the east side of the Jordan, northeast of the Dead Sea. There are ancient traditions locating both of these places, and both appear in the 6th century mosaic map on the floor of a church at Madeba in Transjordan. Finally, there is a town called Salim, four miles east-southeast of Shechem. Eight miles north of this is the village of 'Ainûn. There are springs in its region but not in the town itself.

We do not know whether the evangelist John consciously worked out the geography at this point. But, assuming that he did, he may have thought of Aenon as located in Transjordan, very near Judaea. Alternatively, John may have supposed that Jesus was already on his way to Galilee through the region of Samaria where he met the Samaritan woman and her fellow villagers (4:1-42). John makes one curious remark. Jesus testified that a prophet has no honor in his own homeland (4:44), and Jesus certainly came from Nazareth (1:45). Yet on this occasion the Galileans receive him (4:45). Now Jesus comes to Cana and heals the son of the royal official (4:46-54).

II. Herod's Jerusalem

The next episode in John finds Jesus healing the lame man at the pool of Bethesda.

A pilgrim who visits Jerusalem may be moved by piety or curiosity (or both!) to locate the places where Jesus walked and taught. Such a person has to superimpose an imaginary map on the Jerusalem that is now visible. Maps in guide books are sometimes helpful in this.

The Old City that we see now is enclosed by walls built in the time of Suleiman the Magnificent, the 16th century Turkish sultan. At certain points, especially in the east, these follow approximately the walls of Jesus' time, but not always. Nor do they coincide with the walls in the era of the monarchy of Judah and the time of Ezra and Nehemiah.

The oldest settlement of Jerusalem was outside the Old City and south of the present wall, on the hill called Ophel. This city existed long before David and is the one that he conquered; and even after Jerusalem expanded to the north and west, the Ophel was part of it until the destruction of the city by the Romans.

North of the Ophel was another hill where Araunah the Jebusite, one of the old non-Israelite inhabitants, had a threshing floor. This David purchased as a place to build an altar (2 Sam. 24:18-25). He desired to build a temple also, but this came to pass only in the time of his son Solomon, who also constructed a palace for himself south of the Temple. Later the city spread west and north.

By the time of the Maccabees, Jerusalem included all the area within the present west and south walls. The diagrams in Murphy-O'Connor's book, *The Holy Land,* p. 12, illustrate this. Near the present Citadel, which is just south of the Jaffa Gate, one of the Maccabaean monarchs built a palace.

The city that Jesus knew was laid out by Herod the Great. At this point it is helpful to consider the layout of present day Jerusalem, which is divided into four quarters. In the northeast is the Muslim Quarter which adjoins the Ḥaram esh-Sherif ("noble sanctuary"), formerly the Temple area, now occupied by the Dome of the Rock, the el-Aqsa mosque and a few other Islamic structures. The Christian Quarter (in this instance "Christian" refers predominantly to the Orthodox and Latin Catholic communities) is the northwest quadrant. On the southeast, next to the Ḥaram and extending a little southward, is the Jewish Quarter, which was ruined in the 1948 war and has been largely reconstructed. The Armenian Quarter is the southwestern portion. The gate which leads to it is called Zion Gate because this neighborhood was mistakenly thought in mediaeval times to be David's Zion.

Herod found a sprawling city that had suffered several wars. Apparently he decided to rebuild it on Graeco-Roman lines with two principal streets, one north-south and one east-west. There is evidence that he laid out most other streets on a grid defined by these streets. The whole plan cannot be recovered because it is not possible to excavate the entire city.

The north-south street (Lat. *cardo*) evidently began at the Damascus Gate and continued south along the line of the present Suq or bazaar and beyond the point where the Lutheran Church of the Redeemer now stands. The other main street (*decumanus*) began near the Jaffa Gate and followed what is now David Street, which divides the Christian and Armenian quarters. It continued approximately along the Street of the Chain, north of which is the Muslim quarter.

There is another street that runs south from the Damascus Gate in a southerly and partly easterly direction. This follows an ancient declivity known in Graeco-Roman times as the Tyropoeon ("cheese-makers"). This street is known as el-Wad, the valley. The southern portion of this valley ran along the west wall of the Temple area. At two points streets ran east directly to the Temple wall and were carried on arches over the Tyropoeon street. The remains of these are known as Wilson's arch and Robinson's arch. Mazar's excavations have uncovered a paved section of the Tyropoeon street, far below the present road.

Herod extended an already existing aqueduct to supply the city with water, and built walls and many other structures, including three towers. The lower part of one of these, which he named in honor of his brother Phasael, is probably part of the present Citadel. The other towers, named Hippicus and Mariamme, were nearby. South of these, in the year 23 B.C., when he was 50 years old, he built his palace on or near the site of an old Maccabaean palace.

Herod's crowning architectural work was the Temple. He began this in 19 or 18 B.C. First he constructed immense retaining walls on the west, south and east, and a great stone platform, supported by arches, around the Temple hill to make a level rectangular area. The lower courses of the walls can still be seen, made of huge blocks, some as much as 14 feet long, beautifully cut and perfectly joined.

There was already a temple here which had to be replaced. It was the "Second Temple" built after the Exile (521-516 B.C.), in the time of Zerubbabel and Joshua and the prophets Haggai and Zechariah. All the building materials were assembled before construction began, the regular services were not interrupted, and the workmen were mainly priests and levites.

The whole area was organized as a series of courts. Innermost was the Holy of Holies building on the west. Its east facade was covered with gold plates which were dazzling in the morning sun. The Court of the Priests, east of it, enclosed the altar of sacrifice, on or near the original rock which David purchased. This in turn was surrounded by the Court of the Men of Israel and the latter by the Court of the Women. Around this whole sacred area on three sides, and enclosed by a fence and barriers at each of 13 gates, was the Court of the Gentiles, which anyone might enter.

The ancient rock, which had been Araunah's threshing floor, is now enshrined by the sumptuous and beautiful Dome of the Rock, built by the Ummayad caliph 'Abd al-Malik in A.D. 688-691.

Herod's temple enclosure was surrounded on all four sides by covered galleries. The Royal Stoa on the south was twice as wide as the others. The north wall was evidently a little farther north than the present wall of the Ḥaram. It adjoined the fortress of the Antonia, an older tower which Herod rebuilt early in his reign and named in honor of Mark Antony.

Mazar's excavations have turned up an interesting fact. Many pieces of the stonework decorations of the Temple enclosure have been found, and all the carvings have geometric or floral designs. The biblical law against images of human beings and animals was observed more strictly here than in any other period of Jewish history. Herod was not a good Jew. He built pagan temples in Sebaste (Samaria) and elsewhere, but in constructing the great Jerusalem Temple he had to regard the scruples of the strictest of the Pharisees.

Late in his reign there was a riot because he had arranged to place a golden eagle over the main gate of the enclosure. Zealous students of the Pharisees cut it down.

III. The Pool of Bethesda

It has seemed desirable to give this sketch of Herod's city before locating the place, north of the Temple area, where Jesus healed the lame man. The English translations differ as to whether the Greek means "Sheep Gate" or "Sheep Pool," and variations as to the location of the pool go back to ancient manuscripts. It is at "Bethzatha" in the RSV, Today's English Version, and the Jerusalem Bible, but "Bethesda" in the New English Bible. The manuscripts contain still other variants.

There was a Sheep Gate in the north wall of Jerusalem in Nehemiah's time (445-432 B.C.). In Jesus' day there may also have been a Sheep Pool where sacrificial animals were washed before they were brought to the Temple. Herod's Temple, as we have seen, adjoined the Antonia fortress. The area north of this was evidently a new addition to the city which Josephus called Bezetha, a name whose meaning we do not know. "Bethzatha" might represent an Aramaic word meaning "house of olives."

Variations in the manuscripts suggest that copyists were perplexed by the names they found. Some important manuscripts read Bethsaida and Bethesda; Belzetha is found in a few and may be a variant of Bezetha. "Bethsaida" is probably only the substitution of a well-known name for an obscure one. "Bethesda" has some claim to be the original, for two reasons. (1) The Copper Scroll from Qumran is a curious document which lists the location of various hidden treasures and seems like a piece of wild imagination, but it says that the largest amount of treasure is at a pool which seems to be called Bethesdatain. This word may be translated as "two Bethesdas." (2) "Bethesda" seems to mean "House of mercy," and it would be natural to give this name to a place of healing.

John 5:2 says that the pool or the place had five *stoas* or porticoes. When we consider all of the above, it is interesting to survey the area north of the present Haram and the archaeological discoveries there.

The Antonia fortress is now known to have been located where the Muslim Umariya School now stands. The only gate on the east side of the Old City is known as St. Stephen's Gate because of a late and unreliable tradition that the martyr was stoned near there. One enters through this gate into a street which the Arabs call the Street of our Lady Mary. On the left Herod's masons made the great Pool of Israel to supply water for the Temple. It is now filled in and is occupied by a parking lot. A little farther on is the Umariya School, where Good Friday processions begin, and beyond this the street is known as the Via Dolorosa.

On the right of the parking lot are the monastery of the White Fathers, an order famous for its work in Muslim lands, and also a seminary where the Fathers formerly educated candidates for the Greek Catholic priesthood. A little farther to the north is the exquisite Crusader Church of St. Anne, located where the Virgin Mary's parents, Joachim and Anna, were believed to have had their home. It has been restored to its original simple beauty.

The area north of this church has been excavated, and the House of Mercy must have been here. It is a confusing and tantalizing place. On the west are huge twin pools, partly cut out of bedrock and partly with masonry walls. It has sometimes been guessed that this was the pool of Bethesda because one can imagine five porticoes, four around the perimeter and one between the two pools. But no crippled person could be placed in such a deep cistern. These pools were cut about 200 B.C. by order of the high priest Simon son of Onias, whose fame is celebrated in the deuterocanonical book known as Ecclesiasticus or Sirach (Ecclus. 50:3). The two pools are separated by the bedrock. In Herod's time an east-west street ran over this rock and was integrated into the grid of streets in this part of the city.

East of the pools there is a jumble of ruined masonry, in the midst of which are part of a column and its base, on which crosses are carved. A Byzantine church stood here, and near it there is a small plastered cave and there are signs that there were other caves in the area.

Archaeologists, in reconstructing the history of this site, think that it had been a place of healing long before Jesus' time. We conjecture that there were small pools here, perhaps roofed over by a building with five porticoes, no trace of which has been found. Strict Pharisees probably regarded such healing practices as unorthodox, too much like magic, and in addition, according to the gospel story, Jesus was accused of breaking the Sabbath when he healed this man.

After the second Jewish revolt (A.D. 132-135), Hadrian expelled the Jews from Jerusalem, made it a pagan city, and renamed it Aelia Capitolina. Offerings found on the Bethesda site make it likely that it now became a healing sanctuary like the many medical centres of the god Asklepios throughout the Greek world. We have already mentioned the healing baths at Jewish Tiberias and pagan Gadara.

Later, when Christianity became the official religion of the empire, the Byzantine church was constructed, probably about A.D. 450. This suppressed the pagan associations of the place and was dedicated to the Virgin Mary. The Crusaders found the church in ruins and built a small chapel there as well as the nearby Church of St. Anne.

IV. The Festivals of Passover and Tabernacles

John the Evangelist regularly puts discourses attributed to Jesus after "signs" or miracle stories. The content and language of these speeches are very different from what is found in the other gospels. Many believe that John does not so much report a tradition as to give the miracle a theological interpretation. As his story line goes at this point, the healing at Bethesda leads to a serious confrontation with "the Jews" or "Judaeans" about Jesus' authority and his relationship to his Father (John 5:10-18) and a discourse on these themes (5:19-47).

The end of chapter 4 left Jesus in Galilee; at 5:1 he goes to

Jerusalem for an unnamed festival, which may be Pentecost, because chapter 5 concerns the law and Jesus' interpretation of it, and the rabbis said that the law had been given on Pentecost. Without any explanation, at 6:1 Jesus is in Galilee and crossing the lake to "the other side." It would make some sense if we dared to place chapter 6 between chapters 4 and 5, for the festivals of Passover and Pentecost would be in the right order. There would, however, be the difficulty that Jesus is in Galilee at the beginning of chapter 7. Does John assume a journey of Jesus from Jerusalem to Galilee without mentioning it? Did the author of the gospel die before he finished editing it? There are indications that his disciples put the gospel in its present form (John 19:35; 21:24).

Perhaps it is best to follow the story just as it stands. John now tells of the feeding of the Five Thousand (6:1-15) with some interesting details not found elsewhere. The loaves are made of barley, poor people's bread, and the enthusiastic people want to force Jesus to be their king. Here, as elsewhere in this gospel two questions are raised: Is Jesus the true prophet and king, and what kind of king is he? Then, as in Mark and Matthew, comes the walking on the water (6:16-21).

Jesus' crossing of the lake finds the crowds confused, and this leads to a great discourse in the Capernaum synagogue (6:22-59) in which there are several themes, the meaning of Jesus' "signs," the nature of Jesus, and the manna and the true bread from heaven. Even some of Jesus' disciples have difficulty accepting his words (6:60-66), but Simon Peter, speaking for the Twelve, acclaims him as the Holy One of God, and Jesus alludes to his betrayal by Judas Iscariot (6:67-71). This appears to be John's counterpart to the scene at Caesarea Philippi.

Now in chapter 7 it is early autumn. Jesus' brothers propose to go to Jerusalem for the Tabernacles festival. Our Lord declines to do so, but later he goes there, privately or secretly. This is an indication, as at the marriage in Cana (2:4) that Jesus acts on his own initiative, not at the suggestion of others. He acts at the right time, God's time.

The whole story, and Jesus' words, are symbolic and are connected with the themes of Tabernacles. Every day during this festival the priests conducted a ceremonial pouring out of water, and this was the occasion for Jesus to offer living water (the Spirit, 7:37-39). Apparently the discourse on the light of the world (8:12-20) also belongs to Tabernacles. This was appropriate because at night there were great illuminations, and the worn-out garments of priests were used as wicks in huge bowls of olive oil.

All through this central part of the gospel the hostile confrontation between Jesus and his opponents increases dramatically, and a partial climax comes when the foes pick up stones to throw at him (8:58).

V. The Pool of Siloam

In the next great episode Jesus heals the man born blind (9:1-38). The story develops more than one theological theme. It puts to rest the notion that an illness or physical defect must be the punishment for sin (9:3); the emphasis is on new sight as the glory of God in contrast to spiritual blindness (9:39-41). But it is also a parable of conversion. The man first acknowledges that he is the man who had been healed. When asked about the healer, he says that Jesus is a prophet. Finally Jesus discloses that he is the Son of Man, and the person healed expresses his faith and worships Jesus. As a result, the authorities expel him so that he can no longer be a member of the Jewish community.

Physical means were used in the cure, as in the story of the blind man of Bethsaida, and practices like this were well known in antiquity. Jesus anointed the eyes with clay and saliva (cf. Mark 8:23), and ordered the man to go to the pool of Siloam and wash. John interprets "Siloam" as "sent"; the Hebrew name Shiloah in fact means "the sender." It was water from this place that was used in the ceremonies of Tabernacles; thus it was regarded as pure and appropriate for sacred purposes.

The water came from a spring higher up, to the north.

Christians later called it "the Virgin's fountain," but its Old Testament name was Gihon ("the gusher"). This spring made it possible for the Jebusites, long centuries before David, to build a city on the Ophel hill. They made a tunnel which led to a vertical shaft cut through the solid rock to ensure a supply of water in time of siege. It was evidently this *sinnor* or shaft through which Joab climbed to enter Jebus and capture it for David (2 Sam. 5:8; 1 Chron. 11:6).

Water from this shaft was evidently collected in a pool. This original pool, the *old* pool of Siloam, is now filled up and is a walled garden called Birket el-Hamra, in which fig trees are planted. (*Birkeh* means "pool.") This is at the point where the Tyropoeon valley joins the Kidron valley which runs from the southeast corner of the Temple enclosure.

In Solomon's time Jerusalem was secure, so this monarch was able to make a double use of the Gihon spring. He constructed a channel running along the east side of the Ophel hill which fed the Siloam pool but which also had sluice gates so that gardens along the Kidron valley could be irrigated.

As early as 733-2 B.C., King Tiglath-Pileser III of Assyria attacked Israel (2 Kings 15:29). In the years 705-701 B.C., Jerusalem was in danger from a siege by Sennacherib. King Hezekiah of Judah decided to bring the Gihon waters inside the city wall (2 Kings 20:20; 2 Chron. 32:80). His men cut a tunnel through the rock, 512 metres long (about 1,680 feet), working from both directions. A moment came when the workers on the two sides could hear one another's voices. They broke through and the waters flowed. This was an amazing feat of engineering. It is possible today to walk through the tunnel.

The tunnel ended at a new pool of Siloam, higher up than the previous one. This is still fed from Gihon, but the existing pool occupies only part of the original area.

Perhaps in the time of the emperor Hadrian, this upper pool was covered by a colonnaded structure which was seen by a Christian pilgrim from Bordeaux in 333. Christians believed that this pool was the one to which Jesus sent the blind man, and by the 6th century an "overhanging" church had been built above it.

There is evidence, however, that in Jesus' time it was the lower pool that was in use. Thus the location of the healing is not quite certain.

VI. The Festival of Dedication

All the four gospels have some of the aspects of a tragedy, in that a good man suffers precisely because he is good, persists in following his destiny, and is put to death by the world's powerful forces. Most of the actors in the drama do not realize what is happening, although the spectators (Christians, in this case) are aware. This is dramatic irony. The gospels are not pure tragedy, however, because the story ends in the Resurrection.

John emphasizes these traits. In addition, the conflict between Jesus and his opponents builds up to several high points prior to the story of the Passion. There was conflict at the Tabernacles festival and questions of whether Jesus was the true Messiah.

At one point John says, "Then came the festival of Dedication at Jerusalem; it was winter" (10:22). Tabernacles and Dedication (Ḥannukah) are very similar feasts. The latter, which is celebrated on the 25th day of the Jewish month Chislev, commemorates the rededication of the Temple in 164 B.C. by Judas Maccabaeus after Antiochus IV of Syria had profaned it (1 Macc. 4:36-59; cf. 1:54-61). This festival was originally modelled on Tabernacles, and one reason for the original celebration was that previously the people had not been able to observe the feast of Booths as usual (2 Macc. 10:6-7).

The Gospel of John makes no sharp transition from the one festival to the other. The sections on the light of the world (8:12-20) and freedom (8:31-38) could apply to either, for one of the features of Ḥannukah is the nine-branched candelabrum, which recalls the miracle of the oil that lasted during the festival, and the rededication marked liberty from foreign rule. One is reminded of those symphonies in which one movement merges into the next. Jesus' allegory of the sheepfold and his discourse on the Good Shepherd (10:1-21) are part of the transition.

Confrontation continues, and "the Jews" again are about to stone Jesus (10:31). Our Lord then crosses the Jordan to the place where John had baptized, and other people come to believe in him (10:40-42).

This sets the scene for the greatest "sign" prior to the Cross and Resurrection, the raising of Lazarus (11:1-44). And this is appropriate to the feast of Dedication, for the hallowing of the Temple was a sign of life for the Jewish people after the apparent death of their national and religious life.

VII. The Raising of Lazarus

The miracle occurs not at "Bethany east of Jordan" (1:28) but the village 15 stades (about two miles) from Jerusalem. The town is not mentioned in the Old Testament, and the meaning of its name is uncertain; among the guesses are "house of Hananiah" and "house of the poor."

In the early centuries Christians called the village Lazarion (Lazarus' place) and this name is preserved in its Arabic name el-Azariyeh. There was a church here in the late 4th century, and after it was destroyed by an earthquake a larger one was built in the 5th century. The Crusaders added to it and also constructed a church directly over Lazarus' tomb. By 1400 both of these were in ruins and a mosque had been constructed at the original entrance to the tomb.

The earliest traditions about Bethany are probably those in Mark. After the triumphal entry Jesus looked around the Temple enclosure and then went out to the village to spend the night (Mark 11:11-12). Later he was there in the house of Simon the Leper and an unnamed woman anointed him (Mark 14:3-9). Martha and Mary are first mentioned in Luke 10:38-42 as entertaining Jesus in "a certain village."

By the time the Gospel of John was written the traditions had become complicated. Now it was believed that Mary and Martha had lived in Bethany and that it was Mary who anointed Jesus' feet (John 12:1-8), as the sinful woman had done in Luke 7:36-50.

Bethany

Prior to the writing of John there was probably an old tradition of the raising of Lazarus from the dead, but the story as it stands was written in such a way as to forestall any suggestion that Lazarus had been in a coma and only apparently dead. This objection could have been made to the accounts of the raising of Jaïrus' daughter (Mark 5:21-43) and the young man of Nain (Luke 7:11-17). When Jesus first learns of Lazarus' illness he remains where he is for two days (John 11:6); to walk to Bethany would require an additional day; and when he arrives he is told that Lazarus has been in the tomb for four days (11:17).

The Fourth Evangelist believed that Jesus had the power to restore this man to life, but he did not tell the story for this reason alone. As in all the other signs in this gospel, the purpose is to express a profound theological truth. Thomas is portrayed as an imperfect believer; if the disciples accompany Jesus, he thinks it is only to die with him (11:16). Both the sisters wish that Jesus had arrived sooner. Martha has no doubt of Jesus' power; she believes in the future resurrection and that Jesus is Messiah and Son of God (11:21-27). Yet her faith is not perfect. "The Jews" do not believe at all, and Jesus weeps in indignation (11:33-37). All of this is in contrast to the positive teaching that Jesus gives in this chapter.

The basic proclamation is that Jesus is the resurrection and the life and that one comes into relationship with him through faith. Even if one dies, one is still alive and will not die eternally (11:25-26). Physical death is only a sleep (11:11). Eternal life, therefore, is something that the Christian experiences here and now.

The resurrection of Lazarus is a parable of this. Jesus calls to him and the man responds and comes out. This is the call of the Good News to all Christians. Lazarus is still tied up in the clothing of death; so are all others at the moment when they come to Christ. Therefore, Jesus says, "Untie him and let him go" (11:44). As in the story of the man blind from birth, this miracle symbolizes conversion and also liberation.

VIII. Ephraim

The raising of Lazarus leads immediately to the fatal plot against Jesus' life (11:45-53). The "chief priests" and the Pharisees can see nothing in this event but another miracle that Jesus has performed in order to seize royal power, and in what Caiaphas says there is a fine irony. "It is better for one man to die on behalf of the people so that the whole nation does not perish." Unwittingly he speaks a truth that only the Christians understand.

Jesus now leaves the region of "the Judaeans" and spends some time in "a city named Ephraim" (11:54). A place with this name is mentioned in 2 Sam. 13:23 and this is probably the Aphairema of 1 Macc. 11:34, a few miles northeast of

Bethel. This may be Samieh or et-Taiyibeh. The latter is a Christian village and also a good example of "a city set on a hill" (Matt. 5:14). This passage indicates that some time elapses before Jesus returns to Jerusalem for the last time (11:55). Mary anoints Jesus in Bethany. Lazarus is a danger to the rulers because he can testify to Jesus' power, and they, therefore, plot against him also (12:1-11).

At this point comes the triumphal entry when Jesus is acclaimed as king of Israel. The "Pharisees" ruefully acknowledge that "the whole world has gone after him" (12:18). Again they speak more truly than they know, for now some Greeks come to see Jesus; they symbolize the coming mission to the Gentile world (12:20-22). Philip and Andrew, who have Greek names, are the intermediaries.

This is a sign to Jesus that the hour has now come for the Son of Man to be glorified (12:23). He will be lifted up—in two senses, on the Cross and for the salvation of everyone (12:32). The last part of chapter 12 contains sayings relating to the Church's mission and the unbelief of the Jews, which Isaiah prophesied.

14

The Opposition to Jesus

I

In all four gospels, the hostility of the authorities builds up inexorably toward Jesus' death on the Cross. John stands apart from the other gospels in that the issue is Jesus' authority and his unique sonship to God. Criticisms against his healings on the Sabbath are only incidental to this. The "signs" provoke hostility because they disclose Jesus' power and his authority. Toward the end, however, a political motive emerges even in the Fourth Gospel. The fear is that Jesus will become such a popular leader that he will be proclaimed king. This was foreshadowed at the time when he fed the Five Thousand (John 6:15).

Throughout the other gospels, the anger of the Pharisees was stirred up because of Jesus' independent interpretation of the law. In addition he was criticized because he associated so freely with outcasts. These were reasons for rejecting him but hardly a sufficient motive for plotting his death.

The Pharisees were a large religious party and the most influential in the Jewish community. Their greatest strength was among the middle and lower economic classes, especially in the cities—such people as artisans and merchants. The Pharisees honestly wished to instruct all Jews in proper observance of the sacred law, and through their oral tradition they interpreted the ancient biblical code so as to make it practical and benevolent in a changed social situation. As one great rabbi put it, "Be of the disciples of Aaron, loving mankind and bringing them near to the law." The Pharisees were so successful in this that their program won out and has been the basis of Jewish life ever since.

In the time of the Maccabees they were a political party. They opposed John Hyrcanus I and Alexander Jannaeus because they behaved like kings instead of true high priests. After the death of Jannaeus, his widow Alexandra Salome turned to the Pharisees and they supported her. Herod the Great aimed to reduce the power of the Pharisees and their opponents, the Sadducees, by appointing high priests and other officials who owed their allegiance to him alone. The "Herodians" of the gospels (Mark 3:9; 12:13) were the party that served Herod and his family.

The Sadducees represent an old conservative tradition in Judaism. They rejected the oral law of the Pharisees and apparently held to the letter of Scripture, though they must have had some traditions of their own. They denied the resurrection of the dead. In Jesus' day their strength was among wealthy absentee landowners and a group of priests who controlled the Temple. The high priests Annas and Caiaphas were Sadducees. These people supported the Roman administration, which protected their privileges.

The Pharisees were so numerous that they could not be completely homogeneous. We know from their traditions that their teachers distinguished good Pharisees from others who were half-hearted and cared more for appearance than for the essence of religion. Jesus called the latter "hypocrites," play-actors.

There were at least two prominent "schools" of teaching among the Pharisees, the "house" of Hillel and the "house" of Shammai. Shammai, a Palestinian, was the more conservative. Hillel was an immigrant from Babylonia, more innovative and sensitive to the needs of ordinary people.

After the Jewish War of A.D. 66-73 the Pharisees turned away from political activity altogether, and it is likely that Hillel began this process in Jesus' time. The motive was purely religious. Keeping God's commandments was more important than power; and, from a practical point of view, resistance to the Roman empire would be futile, as later it turned out to be.

Yet, as Josephus tells us, there was a minority group which was like all other Pharisees except that these men favored revolt and hoped to re-establish a theocracy, probably the kind of priestly state that existed under the Persian empire and in the early days of the Maccabees. These are essentially the "zealots" of the gospels. Later they were known as *sicarii* or swordsmen because they assassinated Romans and their collaborators.

The Jewish population of Palestine thus consisted of several groups: non-political Pharisees, Sadducees who collaborated with the occupying power, a small but dangerous number of revolutionaries, the Essenes who were not politically active but who hoped for a victorious war against Rome, and many common people, mostly farmers and villagers who were, so to speak, unattached. Many of these last were religious, but the Pharisees regarded the "people of the land" as uneducated and careless about the law.

II

The situation just sketched sets the stage for Jesus' cleansing of the Temple. Mark is probably correct when he indicates that this occurred toward the end of Jesus' public ministry.

Our Lord had spent the night in Bethany and now entered the Temple area, perhaps through the Huldah gates at the south. He was then in the Court of the Gentiles.

Here the buying and selling took place. Sacrificial animals were always for sale. These had to be inspected by priests and pronounced ritually sound. The rabbinic tradition records protests from the Pharisees that the sellers made exorbitant profits; presumably the priests allowed them a monopoly. Some weeks before Passover, bankers set up their tables to change other coinage into the half-shekel or didrachma in which the annual Temple tax had to be paid. Matt. 17:24-27 tells of a discussion between Jesus and Peter on the subject of this tax.

We have no report of irregularities about this money-changing. But when Jesus drove out the animal merchants the tables of the money changers were overturned (Mark 11:15-19).

Mark adds that Jesus would not permit a vessel to be carried through the Temple area. Evidently it was common practice to use the Court of the Gentiles as a shortcut between two parts of the city. Jesus' action was significant because it implied that the only place where Gentiles could gather was a holy place also.

His words interpreted his actions. "My house shall be called a house of prayer for all the nations." This was a quotation from Isa. 56:7 and expresses one side of Old Testament faith, that Gentiles will be drawn to worship the only true God. Jesus had shown that he identified himself with this sentiment on the relatively few occasions when he came in contact with non-Jews.

"But you have made it a cave of bandits." These words were drawn from Jeremiah's terrible sermon in the Temple (Jer. 7:11). The gist of this was that the people of Judah have had a false trust in the mere fact that they possessed the Temple of the Lord and that, therefore, God would in any case protect Jerusalem. But God would destroy this place as he did to his old sanctuary in Shiloh. The house which bears Yahweh's name has become a cave for bandits. Jesus' quotation implies that the high priest and his gang of confederates are no more than marauders who hide in the Temple, as guerrillas sought out caves in the time of Saul and David, and as they have done in Palestine for times immemorial.

Mark goes on to say that the chief priests and scribes now wished to kill Jesus. They were afraid of him because the crowd was fascinated by his teaching, so for the present they took no action.

What did Jesus intend by this high-handed action? He certainly could not control the Temple precincts except for the moment. His quotations show that, like one of the Old Testament prophets, he was performing a symbolic act. For example, Isaiah went naked and barefoot for three years (Isa. 20), and Jeremiah hid a waistcloth in the cleft of a rock until it was rotten (Jer. 13:1-7). One can only speculate, but when we consider what Jesus did on this occasion, in the light of Jeremiah's Temple sermon, the obvious thought is that unless the nation changes its ways, God himself will come to judgment and even the Temple will not be spared.

Evidently Jesus' final visit to Jerusalem was a last attempt to proclaim God's Reign. He knew the danger and he risked his life.

Whatever his purpose had been when he rode into the city on a donkey, friendly people in Jerusalem made it into a messianic demonstration. The authorities must surely have heard about this, and then when Jesus took control of the Temple precincts the high priest and his friends were convinced that he was about to lead a revolution. The very fact that he had spoken so often of God's Reign was in itself suspicious.

III

From this point on, events moved swiftly. As Mark tells it, Jesus was walking in the Temple area when some of the authorities challenged him by asking, "By what authority are you doing such things?" (Mark 11:27-33). He put them on the horns of a dilemma with a counter-question about the authority of John the Baptist. This implied that Jesus' mission was that of a prophet like John, and thus from God. Since they did not dare to say that John baptized and taught only on his own authority, they responded feebly, "We do not know." Because they could not answer an important and pertinent question, Jesus contemptuously refused to say why he acted as he did.

It would be very natural for Jesus to teach in the Temple, for many people were there every day. Mark makes the Temple the scene of all the teaching in chapter 12. Luke has a special interest in the Temple; all of Jesus' teaching in Jerusalem is located there, and after the Resurrection this is the place where Peter preached.

One of the passages has a direct bearing on Jesus' attitude

to politics and the suspicion of the authorities. This is the dialogue on the paying of taxes to the emperor (Mark 12:13-17). Certain Pharisees and Herodians approached Jesus in an ingratiating way and asked if it were lawful to pay the tax. He answered, "Bring me a denarius; let me see it." This was the silver coin in which Roman soldiers were paid, equivalent to a Greek drachma, and the amount of a common laborer's daily wage. "Whose picture and inscription are on this?" "Caesar's." "Then pay Caesar what is his—and pay God what belongs to God."

The Sadducees would now have found no reason to accuse Jesus of sedition, while the revolutionists would have rejected him at this point. His statement must have pleased most Pharisees, for the emphasis was on allegiance to God's will. In this Jesus gave no positive approval to the empire or any worldly power, for paying God's dues includes the whole duty of men and women. Jesus' loyalty was to the Reign of God, and he carried this out to the end.

IV

A tragedy in the original classical meaning of the word is a story in which the central character comes to ruin and usually death because his conscience or sense of duty puts him or her into opposition with the gods, or the ruler, or destiny. So in Aeschylus' play, Prometheus is chained to a rock because he has defied Zeus in bestowing the gift of fire on mankind. Antigone in the drama by Sophocles buries her dead brother although Creon, the ruler, has forbidden this. Tragedy celebrates the triumph of the human spirit in the face of creaturely limitations, worldly power, or inevitable destiny.

If it were not for the Resurrection, the gospel story would be a perfect example of tragedy. Jesus is in the right, he is as stubborn and single-minded as a tragic hero, and the government brings him to doom. Northrop Frye, in his book *Anatomy of Criticism,* shows that the Passion story also includes much irony, a trait which appears often in tragedy.

The Pharisees and Sadducees, Pilate, and even the disciples do not really know what is going on. Only the spectators, the Christians who read the gospel, know what is actually the case.

Frye also remarks that there are elements of a romantic quest, like the search for the Holy Grail. Jesus has, so to speak, been anointed or commissioned for his journey; this is his baptism. Like a knight, he undergoes testing—the Temptations, which in fact recur in other forms at a later time. He rescues people, confronts enemies, and continues steadily toward his goal, which is to bring his people under God's Rule.

There are even comic touches here and there in Jesus' parables, such as the surly neighbor wakened at midnight, the widow and the Unjust Judge, and the predicament of the Unjust Steward. Jesus has a fine sense of the absurd, as when he tells of a man who wishes to take a speck out of his brother's eye but has a great log sticking out of his own (Matt. 7:3-5).

In the end the story is a comedy, but only in the sense of the word in Dante's *Divina Commedia*. For it ends in Paradise, with Jesus united with the Father and the victory essentially won, even though the world still resists God's Reign.

15

The Last Night

I

The gospels were written to proclaim Jesus as Messiah and Lord, to evoke faith and strengthen it, by telling the great story and preserving the Lord's teaching. They serve the same function today.

To identify the places and study the history, as this book attempts to do, is a proper pursuit. Yet those of us who are Christians can never be detached from the events. In a true sense, they are our history. They tell us who we are and why we are here, and how we can grow into what God intends us to be. The story involves our very lives, and this is supremely true of the narrative of the Passion.

What the gospels recount rests on an oral tradition, some of which had already been written down in shorter documents. Most of the original disciples had already died when the first of the gospels was written. The four evangelists had some interest in history, and they were concerned to show that the great events had actually occurred, but they were not essentially historians. They give a theological, that is, a thoughtful religious interpretation, of the story.

Neither the gospel writers nor the story tellers before them were concerned to satisfy our curiosity by locating each incident and saying of Jesus in place and time. What we have, then, are accounts that have a sound historical basis but which differ in details, and no one can answer for certain all the questions that an historian is bound to ask.

The earliest account of Jesus' last week, that of Mark, (about A.D. 73), orders the events as they might well have occurred, though some of Jesus' teachings could have been given on other occasions.

The Triumphal Entry has always been celebrated on a Sunday, and one reason for this is that the first day of the week is the primary day for Christian worship. Another reason seems to be that all the gospels agree that Jesus was crucified on a Friday. If one takes Mark's account as a basis and works back, the Last Supper was on a Thursday night, and Mark says that this was a Passover night (14:12). He also dates the plot against Jesus, and perhaps Judas Iscariot's betrayal also, two days before Passover; this would be a Wednesday. One may then suppose that the events and teachings of Mark 11:11—13:37 were on Tuesday, that Jesus cleansed the Temple on Monday, and first entered Jerusalem on Sunday (11:11-12, 20).

There is, however, another problem if one considers the Gospel of John. Here the Crucifixion is on a Friday (John 19:31) but this is also the day before Passover, which is a "great Sabbath" (18:28). Jesus, therefore, dies about the time when the paschal lambs were being killed. As St. Paul said, "Christ our paschal lamb has been sacrificed for us" (1 Cor. 5:7). Many scholars, therefore, prefer John's tradition at this point, particularly since when the chief priests and scribes plotted Jesus' death they said they did not want to arrest him during the festival (Mark 14:2).

There have been many attempts to resolve the discrepancy. The most plausible theory is that the evangelist Mark, writing in Rome, depended on a fixed calendar, while in the Holy Land the beginning of the month of Nisan was determined by actual observation of the new moon.

II

The Last Supper certainly occurred on Thursday night. The Jewish day was reckoned from sunset to sunset, and Mark believed that the Passover, the first of the days of unleavened bread, had now begun. Jesus had evidently made secret preparations for the feast because he might be arrested at any time. Two of his disciples were instructed to meet a man carrying a water jug. He would be easily noticed because water was always carried by women, as in Arab villages today. This man would lead them to a "large upper room already furnished" (14:12-16).

Passover was one of the three greatest festivals, essentially a home celebration, and Jesus was to act as father of the family. To this day it is one of the great moments of the year, for it recalls God's protection of the Israelites when the destroying angel passed over the land of Egypt to slay the firstborn. It also commemorates the rescue at the Red Sea and the wandering in the wilderness. Each person present is to think of himself or herself as having participated in these great events and to be identified with the ancient ancestors.

This banquet, however, began with an ominous note. Jesus announced that one of the Twelve would betray him.

At all Jewish dinners there was a thanksgiving over the bread and the wine, with such words as "Blessed art thou, O Lord our God, king of the universe, who hast brought forth bread from the earth ... who hast created the fruit of the vine." The special blessings at Passover are more elaborate.

After the blessings on this occasion, Jesus added the significant words which are regularly repeated in some form in Christian celebrations of the Lord's Supper or Eucharist. "Take this; this is my body." "This is my blood of the covenant which is being shed for many. Truly I tell you, I will no longer drink of the product of the vine until that day when I drink it anew in the Kingdom of God" (14:22-25).

These few words are symbolic and express several thoughts. Jesus is to die, and this death is for the benefit of others. The idea is not strange, for the Jews believed that in the Maccabaean period the martyrs' death liberated Israel. His blood is the blood of the covenant, and this statement recalls the moment when at Mount Sinai Moses read the law to the people, they agreed to obey it, and the covenant was sealed when Moses took half of the sacrificial blood, dashed it on the altar, and threw the remainder on the congregation.

In effect this was a new covenant, a new bond between God and his People (Luke 22:20; 1 Cor. 11:25).

Mark concludes this story by saying, "After they had sung a hymn they went out to the Mount of Olives" (14:26). If this was indeed a Passover, the great Hallel psalms were sung, Pss. 113-114 before the meal and Pss. 115-118 at the end. Early Christians saw in several of these anticipations of the story of Jesus, in particular Ps. 118, which the New Testament quotes more than once.

It is impossible to know, even approximately, where Jesus and the disciples ate the Last Supper. It may have been anywhere in the city, and no early local tradition of it has come down to us.

There is, however, a place called the Cenaculum which later tradition claimed to be the site of the Upper Room. This is the upper story of a building on "Mount Zion," the area south of the present Zion Gate. In the middle ages Christians did not know that the original Zion, that of David, was the Ophel hill. Ophel did not seem to be lofty and important.

South of Zion Gate is the great Benedictine abbey of the Dormition, so named because tradition identified this as the place where the Virgin Mary "fell asleep." The Cenaculum building of which we are speaking is east of this. The lower story contains some ancient walls, and one part of this area is known as the Tomb of David. But David was probably buried on the eastern hill, and the walls may possibly be part of an ancient synagogue.

There is some evidence, however slight, that these walls may be part of the Church of Holy Zion, also called "the Mother of all Churches," because it was believed to be on the site of the "church of God which was small," mentioned in the 4th century by Epiphanius, bishop of Salamis.

Certainly this area was heavily populated in the time of Herod the Great, as we know from excavations between the Dormition and the present city wall. In the middle of the 4th century, St. Cyril of Jerusalem knew a tradition that the Holy Spirit descended on the apostles on Mount Zion (Acts 2:1-4). This was evidently in the "upper room" where Mat-

The two Gethsemane Churches and the Mount of Olives

thias was chosen to take the place of Judas (1:12-26). It would be natural to suppose that this was also the place of the Last Supper, but this identification is not known earlier than the 5th century.

The Valley of Hinnom ("Gehenna") runs southward along the west wall of the Old City and turns east below Mount Zion. It joins the south end of the Tyropoeon valley and then the Kidron. The Kidron is a wady or winter stream between the Temple and the Mount of Olives. After the Last Supper, Jesus and his disciples crossed the Kidron into Gethsemane (John 18:1).

III

The word Gethsemane means "oil-press." In ancient times this area on the lower slopes of the Mount of Olives was probably a large olive orchard. There are a few olive trees in the garden adjoining the Church of All Nations, not as old as the time of Jesus but certainly very ancient.

The road to Bethany and Jericho runs along the east side of the Old City, and a little south of St. Stephen's Gate it bears east for a short distance and then turns south again. At this curve and east of the road there are several holy places.

The first is the Tomb of the Virgin. This is based on a tradition, possibly as old as the 3rd century, that Mary was buried in the Valley of Jehoshaphat (another name for the Kidron valley). The crypt of this church is Byzantine. There are two tombs here, one of which is identified as that of Mary. This has been also a holy place of Islam, and on one wall there is a mihrab or niche pointing in the direction of Mecca. Mary is venerated by Muslims, and Muhammad is said to have seen a light over Mary's tomb.

Next to this structure a passageway leads to a cave, and there are two traditions about this. The disciples were believed to have rested here while Jesus was at prayer; here also Judas Iscariot greeted his Master with a kiss at the time of the arrest.

A little to the south is the Franciscan Church of All Nations or the Church of the Agony, built in 1924. This replaces the ruins of a church built by the Crusaders about 1170. But the earliest church on this spot was constructed between 379 and 384, and the pilgrim Egeria described it as "elegant." The place was chosen because here was a rock on which Jesus was believed to have prayed (Mark 14:32-42). This rock is in the apse of the present church and it was the focal point of all three churches.

No other passage in the gospels is quite like Mark's story of Jesus in Gethsemane, though Matthew (26:36-46) reproduces it substantially and Luke (22:39-46) has some variations. What is most striking is Mark's description of the Lord's emotions (14:33-34); the powerful words are very difficult to translate. Jesus is completely appalled by what he knows will occur, and this comes out clearly.

There is an echo of the Lord's Prayer in 14:36; "Abba (Father), everything is possible with you; remove this cup from me; yet not what I will but what you will." Much earlier Jesus had asked James and John if they could drink the cup that he himself must drink (Mark 10:38). This is the cup of suffering and punishment that is mentioned in the Old Testament (Pss. 11:6; 75:8; Isa. 51:17, 22).

The evangelist John has a different understanding of Jesus' life of prayer. The passage that most closely resembles Gethsemane is in the context of the visit of the Greeks. "Now my soul is troubled," says Jesus, "and what am I to say? 'Father, save me from this hour?' Father, glorify your name." The passage continues: "Then came a voice from heaven, 'I have both glorified it and again will glorify it'" (John 12:27-28).

If there is any inner turmoil in this latter account, it is only momentary. Elsewhere in the Fourth Gospel, Jesus is equally serene. He knows that the time is come for him to depart from this world to the Father, that the Father has given everything into his hands, and that he had come from God and was going to God (13:1-3). The great prayer in Chap. 17 shows him in constant communion with God and looking to the future when the world will believe because of the work of the disciples. When the Temple police come he is completely in control and cannot even be arrested until he gives the word (18:4-11). On the Cross, Jesus does not say "My God, my God, why have you forsaken me?" (Mark 15:34) but "It is finished" (John 19:30); the work of redemption is complete.

The other gospels, and especially Luke, speak of Jesus as praying in solitude, and the Our Father is probably the most characteristic example of his mode of prayer. Every phrase in it is completely Jewish and yet it is marked by his particular interests. Now and then the Synoptic Gospels give possible glimpses into his inner life, as in the Baptism and Transfiguration stories, his vision of the fall of Satan (Luke 10:18), and his thanksgiving to the Father (Luke 10:21 = Matt. 11:25-26), and particularly the tragic words in Luke 12:49-50. But in general they avoid interpretation of his inner thoughts and emotions and are content to record what he did and taught. They do speak of his anger or indignation and his compassion.

Thus the agony in Gethsemane is, if not unique, at least startling. The story we have is told at least partly to stimulate the devotion of Christians. There is equal emphasis on Jesus' sorrow and the failure of his most intimate disciples. They should have kept awake and alert; they should have persisted in prayer.

Jesus had spoken parables about slaves who kept awake, ready for their master's return (Luke 12:35-40 = Matt. 24:45-51; Mark 13:32-37), and the word often translated "Watch" in Mark 13:37 is *grêgoreite*. Gregory ("the alert one") is an honorable name to bestow on a Christian child.

All-night vigils were a feature of Greek paganism. Night prayer was also known among Jews. "At midnight I rise to praise thee"; "My eyes are awake before the watches of the night, that I may meditate upon thy promise" (Ps. 119:62, 148). It was natural, then, that Christians kept vigils, especially at Easter, and the Rule of St. Benedict prescribed a round of psalmody and prayer day and night.

IV

Judas Iscariot now came accompanied by "a crowd with swords and clubs from the chief priests and the elders" (Mark 14:43). These may have been the police, whose duty was to keep order in the Temple, or merely a group of retainers from the high priest's household. One of the slaves of the high priest was among them. "Chief priests, scribes and elders" refers to the Sanhedrin, the religious and civil supreme court, composed of 70 or 72 members, presided over by the high priest, which the Roman administration permitted to have jurisdiction over most cases. It is unlikely that the court as a whole sent these armed men out, but some members of the court may have done so.

There is pathos in the story of Judas' betrayal. Three of the gospels say that Judas received money, but it is hard to believe that this would be a sufficient motive for one of the most intimate disciples, who had eaten and travelled with Jesus, to do such a thing. Luke (22:3) and John (13:2) also ascribe the deed to Satan or the devil. One plausible suggestion is that Judas had hoped that his master would lead a revolution and was bitterly disillusioned. It has even been thought that he wished to put Jesus under protective arrest to preserve him from mob violence.

This was the time of the paschal full moon. There may of course have been clouds; in any case it was dark among the olives, and a signal was needed so that the right man would be taken. So the betrayer greeted Jesus with a kiss. The precautions were needed; there was a scuffle, and someone cut off the ear of the high priest's slave. Jesus taunted his captors for seeking him out as if he were a bandit. They had not had the courage to arrest him in the Temple. This is one indication among several that Jesus had friends in the city.

The captors brought him to the house of the high priest. Caiaphas held this office at the time. His father-in-law Annas, who is also mentioned in the gospels (Luke 3:2; John 18:13, 24), had previously been high priest and was, so to speak, the power behind the throne. Various members of his family were high priests at different times, and a tradition in the Talmud calls them serpents—"the hissing brood of Annas."

We do not know where Caiaphas lived. Late tradition locates his house at the church of St. Peter in Gallicantu ("at the cockcrowing"), but in early centuries a house of Caiaphas was pointed out on Mount Zion near the Dormition. The dwelling probably surrounded a courtyard which was entered through a gate. Peter came in here and tried to keep warm near a charcoal brazier (Mark 14:55).

It seems unlikely that the entire Sanhedrin would be there on the night of Passover, and a trial could not legally be held at such a time. The Mishnah, whose rules may have been in effect at this time, although it was compiled about A.D. 200, provides that a case involving the death penalty must be tried in the daytime and the verdict given in the daytime. One should think of a small group meeting in Caiaphas' residence to conduct an informal inquiry and collect evidence.

First there was a charge that Jesus had uttered a threat against the Temple. His action in the Court of the Gentiles might have been the basis for this, but the witnesses could not agree. The discussion about Jesus' claim to be Messiah is formulated in the light of Christian theology (14:61-65). Apparently he could not deny that in some sense he was the Messiah. This was construed as "blasphemy," although it was not the blasphemy punishable by death. Some time, certainly, Messiah had to come to Israel.

The story of Peter's denial is so vivid that many have thought the great apostle himself had told it to Mark. Who but Peter would tell of his shame? At the same time, the tradition gave hope to ordinary Christians that even one who denied his Lord was able to "turn and strengthen" his brothers (Luke 22:31-32; John 21:15-19).

V

The next scene (Mark 15:1) is a morning meeting of the Sanhedrin, a strange event on Passover day. According to the law, such a session had to take place at the "house of hewn stone," which was in or near the Temple area, possibly a chamber south of the Holy of Holies or just outside the enclosure in an open place called the Xystos. One thinks of a space near the Western or Wailing Wall in present-day Jerusalem as a possible location.

Luke, unlike Mark, puts the examination of Jesus by the high priest at this point (Luke 22:66-71). It is very doubtful that at this time the Sanhedrin had the power to inflict the death penalty. In any case, the Jewish authorities brought Jesus before Pontius Pilate. It was he who sentenced Jesus and he must bear the primary responsibility for this judicial murder. The accusers were able to prevail by interpreting Jesus' messiahship as high treason against the emperor, and our Lord was put to death by the Roman method of crucifixion.

16

The Trial and Crucifixion

I

Pontius Pilate was governor of the imperial province of Judaea. His successors were "procurators," but an inscription found several years ago at Caesarea Maritima on the seacoast, shows that he had the title of prefect, which was also given to the Roman rulers of Egypt. He had his headquarters at this Caesarea, where Herod the Great had built an amazing port city. This governor came up to Jerusalem as need required and probably at festival times, when there was always possibility of trouble. Most probably he stayed at Herod's old palace south of the present Citadel. Herodian masonry has been found there. Mark says nothing about the location except to speak of the "palace" or "praetorium" (15:16). According to Matt. 27:19, Pilate was seated on a *bema* or rostrum, probably in the open air in front of the praetorium or government house (John 18:28). John 18:13 uses the Greek word *lithostroton,* "paved place," and also the Aramaic *gabbatha,* "raised place."

This location is more likely than the Antonia fortress which adjoined the Temple area and which used to be claimed as the place of the trial because of the pavement to be seen in the Franciscan chapel of the Flagellation. The latter is now dated to A.D. 135.

According to Luke 23:2, the accusers made three serious charges against Jesus: misleading the people (perhaps sedition), forbidding payment of taxes to Caesar (demonstrably false), and claiming to be Messiah, a king. This last could amount to treason. Pilate now asked Jesus if he were "the king of the Jews," which was Herod's title, and the answer that has come down to us in Greek might mean "the words are yours." When the accusers made other charges, Jesus was silent. Mark and Luke agree that at this point in the trial Pilate found no reason to condemn him.

II

Luke next inserts an incident that is not found in the other gospels. Pilate sent Jesus to Herod Antipas (23:6-12). This encounter with the tetrarch probably occurred in the old Maccabaean palace which stood west of the Temple area in what is now the Jewish Quarter and overlooked the Xystos. It is not certain whether this was near the western wall of the Temple or nearer the *cardo maximus,* Herod's principal north-south street, which was approximately on the line of the present Street of the Jews. In Byzantine times the Church of Holy Wisdom (St. Sophia) was near here, and this was supposed to be the place where Jesus was flogged.

Luke's account speaks only of Herod Antipas' curiosity. Earlier in the same gospel he had wondered if Jesus were the resurrected John the Baptist (9:7-9). But later the Pharisees had warned Jesus that Herod wished to kill him (13:31). Evidently the traditions have some variety.

Pilate perhaps acted out of courtesy, for Jesus was a Galilean. He may also have expected Herod to provide information about this strange villager, favorable or otherwise. At all events, the tetrarch made fun of Jesus by sending him back in royal clothing. This put an end to the enmity between the two potentates. We do not know how the trouble arose in the first place, but it could have been when Pilate massacred some Galileans as they were offering sacrifice (Luke 13:1-3). As governor of a difficult province, he had been generally successful, for he remained in office ten years. Yet he was occasionally high-handed and he was finally dismissed because of his brutality at Mount Gerizim.

III

The gospels all say that Pilate was reluctant to put Jesus to death and that he offered to follow his policy of releasing a prisoner at this festival. There is no independent evidence that this was his custom, but it would be natural for any governor to evoke good will in this fashion. But a hostile mob instead asked clemency for Jesus Barabbas, as some manuscripts of Matt. 27:16 name him. He was a man who had committed murder during some uprising (Mark 15:7). "Which one do you want, Jesus Barabbas or Jesus the so-called Messiah?" The crowd, probably made up of the high priest's supporters, insisted on Barabbas.

The gospels record the trial before Pilate in different ways. The story in John 18:28-40 portrays Jesus as the true prophet and the king whose realm is not of this world, and he confronts Pilate with the dignity of the Son of God. As the narrative goes on, it also reflects the realities of the political situation. The emperor Tiberius demanded that subject peoples in the provinces should not be exploited too unreasonably or treated savagely, and Pilate knew this. On the other hand, Tiberius had a paranoid fear of treason.

Thus when the accusers said, "If you release this man you are no friend of Caesar" (19:12) and "We have no king but Caesar" (19:15), Pilate gave the verdict. And when later the chief priests protested, "Do not write 'the King of the Jews' but 'He said, I am King of the Jews,'" he was able to insult them: "What I have written I have written." In effect, this is what we will do to any King of the Jews.

IV

Where was Jesus crucified and buried? Since the early centuries, the unanimous tradition has been that Calvary and the tomb were within the great building named the Church of the Anastasis (Resurrection), more commonly known as the Holy Sepulchre. It is only in modern times that this identification has been questioned. The gospels indicate that Jesus was led outside the city (Mark 15:22; John 19:17;

Luke 23:26; Matt. 27:32-33), and Heb. 13:12 says that "he suffered outside the gate." This is altogether likely. The question is where the north and west walls of the city were at that time. The Holy Sepulchre is well inside the present walled city and has been so for many centuries, but what was the situation in the time of Jesus?

Just outside the north wall, between the bus station and the Dominican convent, pilgrims are shown the "Garden Tomb." One who visits Jerusalem for the first time is apt to find this a better place for meditation than the tomb in the Anastasis, which is crowded with chapels and shrines, where priests and monks of several denominations appear to be in competition.

But the Garden Tomb was "discovered" by General George Gordon, the British hero who died fighting in Khartoum. He was visiting the American Colony, which was then a mission in the Old City near the Damascus Gate. Seated on an upper balcony, he looked across the wall and saw a cave in the hill. "That," he said, "is the Place of the Skull." Actually this is an ancient Jewish tomb, and there are others of the same period in the grounds of the Dominican convent of St. Stephen.

Excavations at the Damascus Gate have disclosed the portal of a north wall at that point, but this is as least as late as the reign of Herod Agrippa (A.D. 41-44). It is probable that the traditional Calvary and tomb were actually outside the city, and that the north wall which extended east from a point a little north of the Jaffa Gate, paralleling David Street, turned a right angle to the north and ran parallel to the present Suq street and one block west of it. Herod's enclosed city may not have extended as far north as the Damascus Gate, but it did include as many as three streets north of the Temple area.

V

Jesus was scourged and led away to be crucified (Mark 15:15). Mark goes on to say that the Roman soldiers indulged in some brutal horseplay, dressing Jesus up in a purple robe,

Entrance to the Church of the Holy Sepulchre

placing a crown of thorns on his head, and saluting him as King of the Jews (15:15-20).

Crucifixion was death by torture. A condemned man was forced to carry, not the whole cross but the cross-beam which would be nailed to a pole or tree. On this occasion a man from Cyrene in north Africa, probably a Jew who was on pilgrimage, was required to carry this beam. He was evidently well known to the first readers of Mark's gospel, for the evangelist explains that he was the father of Alexander and Rufus (15:21).

When the Roman general Varus put down the revolt of Judas the Galilean in A.D. 6, he crucified two thousand Jews. The bones of one of these men may have been found a few years ago in a stone ossuary about a mile and a half north of the Old City. The forearms of the victim were nailed to the crosspiece, his heel bones were nailed to an olive wood block affixed to the upright, and his hips were supported by a small seat. The shin bones had been broken.

The torture of crucifixion might go on for hours and even a day or two. The gospels differ as to the actual time of the Crucifixion. Mark speaks of the third hour (15:25), perhaps 7:30 to 9 a.m., while John apparently thinks of a time about noon. Jesus was offered wine mingled with myrrh but rejected it (15:23); pious women often performed this act of mercy. Jesus' agony was relatively brief, for he expired at the ninth hour, after crying out in Aramaic, "My God, my God, why have you forsaken me?" (15:34, 37). It is possible that as he hung on the Cross he had been meditating on the 22nd Psalm. The opponents had mocked him, but a centurion standing nearby was impressed by Jesus' loud shout and exclaimed, "Truly this man was a son of God."

VI

A remnant of the traditional rock of Calvary stands in chapels to the southeast of the Sepulchre itself. In the 1st century most of this rock had been quarried away, but its upper part can be seen by ascending stairs just inside the main door of the church. The base is in the Latin and Greek chapels, which are on a lower level.

The present form of the Church of the Anastasis is essentially the work of the Crusaders, who in the 12th century restored and expanded earlier structures. Their church was damaged by fire in 1808 and by an earthquake in 1927. Beginning in 1959, the Latin, Greek and Armenian communities have restored most of its earlier glory. The work was done by the excellent local Arab masons.

The church is essentially the cathedral of the Greek Orthodox patriarch, but the Catholics, Armenians, Syrians, Copts and Ethiopians have traditional rights within it. For some centuries its official custodian has been a Muslim, whose office belongs to a certain family.

The church has two principal parts, a rotunda on the west which surrounds the Holy Sepulchre, and the main church whose style is transitional between Romanesque and Gothic. East of the apse, steps lead down to the chapel of St. Helena. Near this is the cistern where the empress was believed to have found the True Cross.

The monument enshrining the tomb itself is an ugly 19th century affair, built after the fire had destroyed an earlier structure. It is one of the paradoxes of religious history that this place for prayer and meditation has suffered at the hands of Christ's worshippers as well as those of his enemies.

Yet we believe that there is a continuity. There is a tradition that Christians worshipped at this spot in the 1st century and remembered where it was even after the emperor Hadrian made Jerusalem a pagan city in A.D. 135.

The area had originally been a quarry. Part of the Calvary rock was left untouched because it was cracked and not suitable for building purposes. The unquarried portion also included tombs cut into the living rock. There are several examples of such burial places in and around Jerusalem. The "Tombs of the Kings" illustrate how a circular stone was rolled through a groove to close a tomb chamber. The tombs of "Absalom" and others in the Kidron valley are of a different type. Here the surrounding rock has been cut away so as to create an impressive, free-standing monument.

The sepulchre of Jesus was evidently one of the cave tombs in the quarry area. At Hadrian's orders this entire area was filled in to provide a foundation for a new pagan temple. St. Jerome believed that the purpose of the emperor was to obliterate all traces of Christianity. More probably his plan was to provide a magnificent place of worship for the Gentile city which he renamed Aelia Capitolina. This was to manifest the power of the empire and its devotion to its gods. The temple would be in a prominent place with easy access from the city's main street.

Eusebius says that a shrine of Aphrodite was built over the cave (*Life of Constantine* vii. 26), but according to Jerome, a statue of Jupiter (Zeus to the Greeks) stood on the tomb of Jesus while one of Venus (Aphrodite) was on the rock of Calvary. This would suggest that the temple may have been in honor of the Capitoline triad, Jupiter, Juno and Minerva. The temple is represented on one of Hadrian's coins and contains figures of these three deities.

In Hadrian's time this was now inside the walled city. In the excavations beneath the Russian Mission in Exile, just north of the Church of the Redeemer, there is masonry which was probably part of the retaining wall of the temple.

Constantine the Great was determined to build a Church of the Resurrection, as he also built the church in Bethlehem and one on the Mount of Olives. The local Christians affirmed that this was the exact place; therefore he demolished the pagan structure and uncovered the tomb of Jesus. Beginning in 326, he constructed a basilica with an apse, an open courtyard with the rock of Golgotha at its southeast, and the tomb. The cliff was cut away so that the tomb chamber could stand free. Using pictures from pilgrim flasks of the 6th century and a 10th century stone model, John Wilkinson has shown what the tomb probably looked like in the 4th century.

The church was set on fire by the Persians in 614 and later repaired. When the Muslim armies captured Jerusalem in 638, the caliph Omar respected this Christian holy place, but a later fanatical caliph, Hakim, in 1009 destroyed the church and most of the tomb. The Byzantine emperor Constantine Monomachos restored the church partially, but the nave was much reduced in size. The Crusaders required fifty years to produce the present basilica.

VII

The man who took Jesus' body from the Cross was named Joseph, an honorable or wealthy member of the Sanhedrin who came from Arimathaea. This town was evidently located in the foothill country ten miles northeast of Lydda and may be the same as Ramathaim-zophim, where the prophet Samuel was born (1 Sam. 1:1). Luke 23:51 says that he had not joined in the condemnation of Jesus, and John 19:38 and Matt. 27:57 that he was a disciple. He may, however, have been at this time only a conscientious man who hoped for the Kingdom of God (Mark 15:42-46).

To bury the dead was always a pious act (Tobit 1:16-18), and this was a festival time when dead bodies should not be exposed. Joseph bought a linen cloth, placed the body in the sepulchre and rolled the disk-shaped stone to close the entrance (Mark 15:46). If it was a new tomb, not previously used (Luke 23:53; John 19:41), it may be that Joseph had intended it for the use of his own family (Matt. 27:60).

The earliest tradition is that Mary Magdalene, Mary of James and Salome brought spices for embalming (Mark 16:1), but John gives this honor to Nicodemus (19:39). This was evidently on Sunday morning.

17

The Resurrection and Ascension

I

Although the accounts of the Resurrection differ considerably in details, they all agree in the fundamental Christian conviction, which is affirmed throughout the New Testament, that Christ was raised from the dead on the "third day," Sunday.

Paul, the earliest to write of this, makes no allusion to the empty tomb, but the gospels, beginning with Mark 16:1-8, make this the basis of their story. What Paul emphasizes is that the glorified Lord was actually seen, first by Peter (1 Cor. 15:5), and Luke also has this tradition (24:34). But—except in the Gospel of John—it is Mary Magdalene and the other women who had stood near the Cross, who otherwise are so seldom mentioned in the gospels, who were the first to find the sepulchre empty and to have news of the Resurrection. In fact, according to John, Mary is the first actually to meet Jesus (20:11-17; cf. Matt. 28:9-10, where the women encounter him).

These discrepancies, although they have some interest, do not affect the basic testimony of disciples of Jesus that they were convinced they had met and spoken with the risen Lord. So many were the experiences in the first few hours and days that the tradition came down in various forms. The tradition does not "prove" the truth of the Resurrection to a skeptic, but it does establish the fact of the disciples' faith.

And instead of acting hysterically they went out to spread the news. Out of their conviction there developed the Christian faith in Jesus as risen, ascended and ruling over his Church.

St. Paul, who is the earliest writer to mention the Resurrection (1 Cor. 15:1-11), says nothing about where the risen Lord was seen. There are two sets of traditions in the gospels. Mark 16:7 promises a reunion of Jesus and his disciples in Galilee, and in Matt. 28:16-20 and John 21 he appears to them there. The other tradition records appearances in Jerusalem and Judaea (Luke 24:13-53; John 20:1-29; Mark 16:9-20, which is apparently an appendix by another and later writer; cf. also Matt. 28:9-10). In John 20:19 the disciples are in a room with the door closed, and in Luke 24:41-43 Jesus eats with them. After the Ascension, the Eleven and Mary, the mother of Jesus, are in an "upper room" (Acts 1:12-14), and the evangelists may think of the Upper Room of the Last Supper as the place where the Lord appeared.

One account that is surpassingly beautiful is the story of how Cleopas and another disciple (a friend or his wife?) walked with Jesus to Emmaus (Luke 24:13-35). This is especially significant because it gives a glimpse into the religion of the earliest Christians. It is the risen Jesus himself who opens the Scriptures up to them and so interprets the Cross and Resurrection. Throughout the new Testament we find Christians understanding passages in the Old Testament as pointing toward Christ. They no doubt believed that as they read the sacred text Christ spoke to them through the Spirit. The unique feature in the Emmaus story is that they recognized Jesus in the "breaking of the bread," which is Luke's way of mentioning the Lord's Supper. Ancient Christians discerned the spiritual presence of Christ in worship. They also expected to see visions, and sometimes they did so.

Where was Emmaus? Most manuscripts of Luke 24:13 say that it was 60 stadia from Jerusalem, about seven miles. Two of the traditional sites fit this distance. One is Abu Ghosh, the Kiriath-jearim of the Old Testament, on the main road from Jerusalem to Tel Aviv. The Crusaders may have chosen this village because it was on the highway they knew and the place nearest to a point 60 stadia from the city. The other, el-Qubeibeh, is north of here on another, less travelled, road. In the 12th century a church and castle were constructed here, perhaps to provide a place where pilgrims could rest on their way to the Holy City. The church, reconstructed in 1902, is attractive, but the site has been identified as Emmaus only since about 1500.

In ancient times there was a city named Emmaus near the coastal plain, which figured in the wars of Judas Maccabaeus (1 Macc. 3:38—4:15). In the 3rd century A.D. it was renamed Nicopolis, but its modern Arabic name is Imwas. A tradition as early as Eusebius in the 4th century regarded this as the Emmaus of the gospel story, and the Christian scholar Julius Africanus lived there. A Byzantine church (perhaps 5th century) was located in the town; later the Crusaders built a smaller church, using the old apse.

The difficulty is that Emmaus-Nicopolis is much farther from Jerusalem than the other places. But there are a few ancient manuscripts of Luke 24:13 that read 160 stadia, and Eusebius and Jerome accept this reading, as do the Armenian and Palestinian Syriac translations.

The Cistercian abbey of Latrun is nearby. The story is that two of the monks once decided to see if it was possible to walk from Jerusalem to Imwas and back again in the evening. They were successful.

II

The earliest tradition seems to have considered the Resurrection and Ascension as a single event, or in immediate proximity. The ending of Luke's gospel (24:50-53) says that on the day of the Resurrection Jesus led the Eleven "as far as Bethany," where he blessed them "and was carried up into heaven," although a few important manuscripts omit the latter words.

It may, however, be that Luke makes a distinction between Jesus' final appearance to human beings in the Ascension story of Acts 1:6-11, and Jesus' return to his father and his exaltation in glory. Paul seems to regard his own experience of seeing the risen Lord as an exceptional event, for he describes himself as an "abortion" (1 Cor. 15:8). It is significant that Jesus, in speaking to Mary Magdalene, says, "Do not hold on to me, for I have not yet ascended to my Father" (John 20:17). This concept of the Ascension as exaltation is found also in John 13:1; 16:10; 17:11; Luke 22:69; and Acts 2:34-36.

The Christians of Jerusalem would naturally ask where the Ascension occurred. Luke's gospel had mentioned Bethany, and Acts 1:12 says that after the Ascension the disciples returned to Jerusalem from the Mount of Olives, a sabbath day's journey, perhaps a little less than a mile.

When Constantine built churches in the Jerusalem neighborhood it was to enshrine three caves, the Nativity grotto at Bethlehem, the Holy Sepulchre, and a cave on the side of the Mount of Olives. There is tradition in the Apocryphal Acts of John that on the day of the Crucifixion the Lord appeared to John in such a cave, taught him the meaning of the Cross, and then ascended. According to other traditions it was here that he predicted the future tribulation and the coming of the Son of Man (Mark 13; Matt. 24; Luke 21:5-36).

As in Bethlehem and Jerusalem, Constantine designed this church so that the apse was above the cave. This has been reconstructed as a roofless building which outlines part of the original church, which adjoins the Carmelite convent and the Church of the Pater Noster. In the middle ages the tradition was that here Jesus had taught the disciples the Lord's Prayer, and the cloister is decorated with tiles that give the prayer in 62 languages.

Later piety settled on an open space rather than a cave as the site of the Ascension. The famous pilgrim Egeria, to whom we are indebted for so much information about 4th century Jerusalem, joined in a celebration of the Ascension in 384. This was on a small hill a little farther up the Mount of Olives. About six years later a pilgrim named Poemenia, who belonged to the imperial family, had a circular colonnade constructed around a courtyard open to the sky. The

Chapel of the Ascension on the Mount of Olives.

rock of the Ascension was in the centre of this. On it is a mark which was believed to have been made by Jesus' right foot. A mediaeval building with a dome now stands over the rock. Muslims believe in Jesus' ascension and the sacredness of the place, and adjoining the area there is a mosque with its minaret.

III

Most ancient people believed in a universe that was three-tiered, with heaven up above and Hades or Sheol underneath. Greek scientists had, however, known for a long time that the earth was round. Herodotus tells of Phoenicians who circumnavigated the African continent, yet not everyone believed the story. Eratosthenes in the 3rd century B.C. calculated the circumference of the earth with only a slight error, but this information did not affect the world-view of the general population.

Even in modern times the discoveries of Galileo and Copernicus were not accepted quickly. To deny that the earth was flat seemed to contradict the "truth" of the Bible, and not all theologians were as acute as Cardinal Bellarmine (1542-1621) who made a remark something like this: "Scripture does not tell us where heaven is but how to get there."

Christian believers now do not seem to have difficulty in revising their thinking about the Ascension. A hymn by Howard Chandler Robbins expresses it this way:

> And have the bright immensities
>   Received our risen Lord,
> Where light-years frame the Pleiades
>   And point Orion's sword?
> Do flaming suns his footsteps trace
>   Through corridors sublime,
> The Lord of interstellar space
>   And conqueror of time?
>
> The heaven that hides him from our sight
>   Knows neither near nor far;
> An altar candle sheds its light
>   As surely as a star;
> And where his loving people meet
>   To share the gift divine,
> There stands he with unhurrying feet,
>   There heavenly splendors shine.

BIBLIOGRAPHY

The literature is vast, and this is only a selection to provide further information on matters discussed in the text.

I. GUIDE BOOKS

Many guide books are available, both simple and more detailed. Some are designed for readers interested in present-day Israel and Jordan. Others, like those listed below, concentrate on places important in history from the earliest times until now.

Jerome, Murphy-O'Connor, O.P., *The Holy Land.* Oxford University Press, 1980. An archaeological and historical guide, arranged by localities.

John Wilkinson, *The Jerusalem Jesus Knew.* London: Thames & Hudson; New York: Thomas Nelson and Sons, 1978. Principally 1st century Jerusalem, with some attention to the history and geography of all Palestine.

J. Robert Terrigo, *The Land and People Jesus Knew.* Minneapolis: Bethany House, 1985. Illustrated; very brief text.

II. GEOGRAPHY AND ATLASES

Good atlases usually contain historical and geographical information (geology, climate, agriculture, etc.) along with the necessary maps. The following is a selection.

J.B. Pritchard (ed.), *The Harper Atlas of the Bible.* San

Francisco: Harper & Row, 1987. The most recent; very complete. Also published in London as *The Times Atlas of the Bible*.

H.G. May (ed.), *Oxford Bible Atlas*, 3rd ed. Oxford University Press, 1984.

L. Grollenberg, O.P., *Atlas of the Bible*. London: Thomas Nelson, 1958.

Y. Aharoni and M. Avi-Yonah, *The Macmillan Bible Atlas*, revised ed. New York: Macmillan, 1977.

Dan Bahat, *Carta's Historical Atlas of Jerusalem*. Jerusalem: Carta, 1983.

Denis Baly, *The Geography of the Bible*, revised ed. New York: Harper & Row, 1974.

T.A. Collins and R.E. Brown, "Biblical Geography," *The Jerome Biblical Commentary*, pp. 633-652. Englewood Cliffs, N.J.: Prentice-Hall, 1968.

Sir George Adam Smith, *The Historical Geography of the Holy Land*. New York: Harper & Row, 1966, and many earlier editions.

Nelson Glueck, *The River Jordan*. Philadelphia: Westminster, 1946.

III. ARCHAEOLOGY

The Interpreter's Dictionary of the Bible (=*IDB*). 4 vols., New York: Abingdon Press, 1962; Supplementary Volume, 1976. Contains archaeological data in several articles on specific sites, and also a general article on "Archaeology," I, 195-207.

Biblical Archaeology Review (=*BAR*). Some articles are listed below, referring to specific sites.

The Biblical Archaeologist, published by the American Schools of Oriental Research. A little more technical.

Raymond E. Brown, S.S., *Recent Discoveries and the Biblical World.* Wilmington, Del.: Michael Glazier, 1983.

H. Shanks and B. Mazar, *Recent Archaeology in the Land of Israel.* Washington, D.C.: Biblical Archaeology Society, 1984.

Y. Aharoni, *The Archaeology of the Land of Israel.* Philadelphia: Westminster, 1982.

IV. THE LIFE OF JESUS

Books on the life of Jesus are published every year, from every possible point of view. Many are uncritical and reflect fantastic private opinions. The books selected represent good contemporary scholarship and are serious attempts to understand Jesus historically, and often theologically.

G. Bornkamm, *Jesus of Nazareth.* New York: Harper, 1960. Perhaps the best example of recent German Protestant scholarship.

G.S. Sloyan, *Jesus in Focus.* Mystic, Conn.: Twenty-Third Publications, 1983. A modern and reverent approach to various New Testament perspectives on the story of Jesus.

Geza Vermes, *Jesus the Jew.* Philadelphia: Fortress, 1985. Vermes is an eminent Jewish scholar who attempts to see Jesus in his contemporary setting.

V. GOSPEL STUDY

Jan Lambrecht, S.J., *The Sermon on the Mount: Proclamation and Exhortation.* Wilmington, Del.: Michael Glazier, 1985.

Augustine Stock, O.S.B., *Call to Discipleship: A Study of Mark's Gospel.* Wilmington, Del.: Michael Glazier, 1982.

Mark Link, S.J., *The Seventh Trumpet*. Niles, Ill.: Argus Communications, 1976. Useful for orienting the general reader to the nature of the gospel tradition.

Proclamation Commentary series, published by the Fortress Press, Philadelphia.

J.D. Crossan, *In Parables*. San Francisco: Harper & Row, 1973. Important for understanding the symbolic nature of Jesus' language.

N. Perrin, *Rediscovering the Teaching of Jesus*. New York: Harper & Row, 1967. Concentrates on the parables.

VI. INFORMATION ON SPECIFIC SITES

Chapter 1
IDB, I, 394 f.; Suppl. 97.

Chapter 2
IDB, III, 524-526.

Chapter 3
IDB, II, 344-350.

Chapter 4
IDB, IV, 639 f; *BAR*, X, 3 (1984), 32-44.

Chapter 5
IDB, III, 221; Suppl. 561; *BAR*, X, 3 (1984), 22-31.

Chapter 7
IDB, I, 532-534, Suppl. 140 f.; *BAR* IX, 1 (1983), 24-31; *VII, 6 (1982), 26-37; XIII, 5 1987), 22-36.*

Chapter 8
IDB, I, 396 f.; II, 335, 382-384; *Christian News from Israel, n.s.; XXII, 2 (6) (1971), 72-76.*

Chapter 9
IDB, I, 480; II, 584; III, 500; IV, 508 f.

Chapter 10
IDB, IV, 182-188, 313-315; Suppl. 771 f., 776, 821 f.

Chapter 11

Jericho: *IDB*, II, 835-839; Suppl. 412 f. J.R. Bartlett, *Jericho*. Grand Rapids: Eerdmans, 1983.
Jordan: *IDB*, II, 973-978.
Dead Sea: *IDB*, I, 788-790.
Qumran: *IDB*, I, 790-802. P.R. Davies, *Qumran*. Grand Rapids: Eerdmans, 1983.

Chapter 12

John Wilkinson, *The Jerusalem Jesus Knew*, pp. 109, 113-117.

Chapters 13-15

Aenon: *IDB*, I, 52.
Bethany: *IDB*, I, 387 f. Wilkinson, pp. 108-112.
Ephraim: *IDB*, II, 121.
Jerusalem: *IDB*, II, 843-866; Suppl. 475-477. Dame Kathleen M. Kenyon, *Digging Up Jerusalem*. New York: Praeger, 1974. N. Avigad, *Discovering Jerusalem: Recent Archaeological Excavations in the Upper City*. Nashville: Thomas Nelson, 1983.

Chapters 16-17

IDB, Suppl. 199 f.; *BAR*, XI. 1 (1985), 44-53; XI, 6 (1985), 20f.; XII, 2 (1986), 22-57; Wilkinson, pp. 144-197.

Appendices

CHRONOLOGICAL TABLE

B.C.

ca. 1375	Beginning of Amarna correspondence
ca. 1300-1250	Exodus from Egypt
ca. 1225-1200	Joshua's conquest
ca. 1150-1020	Period of Judges
ca. 1020-1000	Saul
ca. 1000-965	David, king in Hebron and Jerusalem
ca. 965-931	Solomon, king
ca. 874-853	Ahab, king of Israel
ca. 722	Fall of Samaria
ca. 587	Fall of Jerusalem
ca. 538	Jews begin to return from Exile
ca. 520	Temple in Jerusalem rebuilt
333	Alexander the Great defeats Persians at Issus
305-198	Egyptian (Ptolemaic) rule in Palestine
198-ca. 129	Syrian (Seleucid) rule in Palestine (after 164 only partially)
164-63	Maccabaean dynasty (complete control after 129)
63	Pompey captures Jerusalem
40	Parthians and Antigonus invade Palestine; Herod appointed King of the Jews
39-37	Herod gains control over Palestine
20	Herod begins to build the new Temple
ca. 8-6	Birth of Jesus Christ
4	Death of Herod

A.D.

ca. 28-29	Beginning of Jesus' ministry
30	Probable year of Jesus' crucifixion
66-73	First Jewish revolt
73	Fall of Masada
130-135	Second Jewish revolt

TABLE OF RULERS

Maccabaean Rulers

Judas Maccabaeus, 166/165-160
Jonathan, 160/159-142
Simon, 142/141-135/134
John Hyrcanus I, 135/134-104
Aristobulus I, 104-103
Alexander Jannaeus, 103-76
Salome Alexandra, 76-67
Aristobulus II, 67-63
Hyrcanus II, 63-40
Antigonus Mattathias, 40-37

Members of Herodian Family and Roman Rulers

Herod the Great, King of the Jews, 40-4 B.C.
Archelaus, Ethnarch of Judaea, 4 B.C.-A.D. 6
Herod Antipas, Tetrarch of Galilee and Peraea, 4 B.C.—
  A.D. 39
Philip, Tetrarch of Ituraea and Trachonitis, etc., 4 B.C.—
  A.D. 34
Prefects/Procurators of Judaea, A.D. 6-41
  Pontius Pilate, A.D. 26-36
Herod Agrippa I, King, A.D. 41-44 (from 37, King also over
  the tetrarchy of Philip)
Procurators, A.D. 44-66
Herod Agrippa II, King of various regions, A.D. 53-93

Roman Emperors

Augustus, 27 B.C.-A.D. 14
Tiberius, A.D. 14-37

Gaius (Caligula), 37-41
Claudius, 41-54
Nero, 54-68
Galba, Otho, Vitellius, 68-69
Vespasian, 69-79
Titus, 79-81
Domitian, 81-96
Nerva, 96-98
Trajan, 98-117
Hadrian, 117-138

ARCHAEOLOGICAL PERIODS

Most archaeological dating prior to the Hellenistic period is based on pottery, and experts do not always agree. These tables represent the most recent consensus for Palestine.

B.C.	
8300-6000	Pre-pottery Neolithic (Jericho)
6000-5000 or 4800	Neolithic
5000 or 4800-3150	Chalcolithic
3150-2200	Early Bronze
2200-1550	Middle Bronze
1550-1200	Late Bronze
1200-1000	Iron I
1000-586	Iron II
586-332	Babylonian and Persian (Iron III)
332-37	Hellenistic
37 B.C.-A.D. 324	Roman

Note. The Bronze and Iron ages are usually divided into sub-periods.

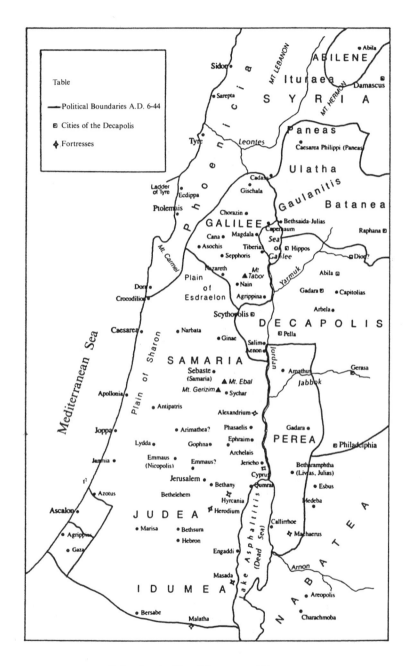

Palestine in New Testament Times

Index

Old Testament

New Testament

Other Jewish Writings

Josephus, *Jewish War*

Other Christian Writings